SPANNING THE
Abyss

Also by Ángel Manuel Rodríguez:

Future Glory

To order, call **1-800-765-6955**.

Visit us at **www.reviewandherald.com**
for information on other Review and Herald® products.

SPANNING THE Abyss

*How the
Atonement Brings
God and Humanity
Together*

Ángel M. Rodríguez

REVIEW AND HERALD® PUBLISHING ASSOCIATION
Since 1861 | www.reviewandherald.com

Review and Herald® titles may be purchased in bulk for educational, business, fund-rais-
ing, or sales promotional use. For information, please e-mail
SpecialMarkets@reviewandherald.com.

The Review and Herald® Publishing Association publishes biblically based materials for
spiritual, physical, and mental growth and Christian discipleship.

The author assumes full responsibility for the accuracy of all facts and quotations as cited
in this book.

Unless otherwise noted, Bible texts in this book are from the *Holy Bible, New
International Version.* Copyright © 1973, 1978, 1984, International Bible Society. Used by
permission of Zondervan Bible Publishers.

Scripture quotations marked NASB are from the *New American Standard Bible,* copy-
right © 1960, 1962, 1963, 1968, 1971, 1972, 1973, 1975, 1977, 1994 by The Lockman
Foundation. Used by permission.
Bible texts credited to NRSV are from the New Revised Standard Version of the
Bible, copyright © 1989 by the Division of Christian Education of the National Council
of the Churches of Christ in the U.S.A. Used by permission.

This book was
Edited by Gerald Wheeler
Copyedited by James Cavil
Designed by Trent Truman
Cover credits
    Cross of clouds: © Marion Wear / 123RF
    Crown of thorns: © iStockphoto.com / Lisa Thornberg
Interior designed by Heather Rogers
Typeset: Times New Roman 10.5/13.5

PRINTED IN U.S.A.

12   11   10   09   08   5   4   3   2   1

Library of Congress Cataloging-in-Publication Data
Rodriguez, Angel M. (Angel Manuel)
    Spanning the abyss: how the atonement brings humanity and God together /
Angel Manuel Rodriguez.
        p. cm.
1. Atonement. 2. Atonement—Biblical teaching. 3. Trinity. 4. God (Christianity).
I. Title.
BT265.3.R63 2008
232'.3—dc22
2008005139

ISBN 978-0-8280-2357-3

LOVINGLY Dedicated to

Edlyn Enid

May the saving

and transforming power

of the cross of Jesus

constantly enrich you

and your family.

Contents

INTRODUCTION

God has done the indescribable. We may not be able to comprehend it fully, but we can enjoy its full benefit. Through self-sacrifice, manifested in the incarnation, ministry, and death on the cross of His only Son, He repaired humanity's rebellious break from the loving harmony of His universal rule. In doing that most painful act of redemption, He also brought to an appropriate solution the cosmic conflict between good and evil, God and Satan. That work of the Lord on behalf of His creatures is called in Christian doctrine the atonement. The history of Christian theology has seen many attempts to uncover the meaning of the atonement, but none of the theories proposed has found universal acceptance. The depth of the subject as well as the large amount of information found in Scripture on the topic make it difficult to formulate a fully integrated interpretation of the doctrine. Many dimensions of the atonement escape human understanding and cannot be forced into a rationalistic system of thought. For instance, no matter how much we may say about the Incarnation, it will always remain beyond us. The same applies to the impact of the death of Christ on the inter-Trinitarian relationships. Those events and experiences are located at the very core of the atonement.

Christians from all denominations continue to debate the meaning of the cross. We witness a strong reaction against the substitutionary understanding of the death of Christ, and many Christians are abandoning it. Some see the cross as a symbol that encourages the abuse of the weak or as supporting systems of oppression. The main attack has come from feminist theologians who argue that the cross, when interpreted as the Father punishing the Son, inflicting pain on Him, and finally killing Him in order to save sinners, reinforces victimization, places at the center of the gospel violence in social relationships, and validates oppression by the powerful. These are serious charges that require Christians to make sure that they present the doctrine of the atonement in a way that is truly a glorious revelation of the love of God that seeks to bring to an end all violence.

Adventists also debate the subject of the meaning of the cross and how we are saved through it. We should not discourage that, but we should evaluate what we place on the Adventist table at the light of Scripture. Some of the interpretations offered deny important biblical aspects of the atonement that we should affirm. Others take us beyond the biblical realm into human speculations that threaten to distort other biblical doctrines. Those advocating different views sometimes present them as the exclusive biblical understanding of the meaning of the cross. Their proponents often call the church to proclaim their own particular understanding of the atonement as the right one. Such debates will continue among us.

However, Scripture has revealed enough to make the doctrine intelligible and, more important, existentially meaningful to us. In fact, the most significant aspect of the atonement is not developing a logically sound understanding of it, but experiencing its saving power in our lives. We should—and we can—affirm in full confidence that through the sacrifice of Christ our sins have been forgiven and we have been reconciled with God. We have the peace that comes to those who have been justified by the precious blood of the Lamb! That is what the atonement is all about.

In what follows we will examine much biblical evidence addressing the subject of the atonement. Recognizing the complexity of the topic, we have chosen to allow the biblical richness to express itself without trying to force it into a particular model of the atonement. We will emphasize the sacrificial and substitutionary dimension of the atonement because it appears throughout Scripture and the church has rightly embraced it, but at the same time we will incorporate insights from many other models into our exposition. I will particularly examine the involvement of the Godhead in the atonement because it is an aspect that has not been seriously explored. Needless to say, what I offer are suggestions for discussion and analysis, hoping that they will lead to a response of gratitude to God for what He has done for us through His Son. The study of this topic should lead us to worship and to a closer walk with the Lord in a spirit of service to Him and to others. We should try to understand as much as possible the doctrine of the atonement, make sure that we have appropriated its benefits, and then proclaim it to others who have not yet found in Christ their Savior and Lord.

1

THE GOD OF THE
Atonement

Quite often the beginning determines the final destination. This is particularly the case when we delve into the world of ideas and theological analysis. In our particular case, where we begin the study of the atonement will practically establish where we will end up. Hence, the first question we should address is one of beginnings—that is to say, What is our starting point and what is it that we take with us as we initiate our study of the topic? Our concern with a proper beginning, however, does not preclude the element of surprise or being able to find the unexpected. In fact, a proper point of departure could lead us through unexpected paths or at least through areas that could challenge our preconceived ideas and deepen our understanding of the subject at hand.

Point of Departure in the Doctrine of the Atonement

So where should we begin our study of the atonement? Since I am a Christian, I start my analysis with the faith conviction that only the Scriptures provide for us reliable, trustworthy information about the doctrine of the atonement. Through searching them we can make meaningful and true statements about the subject. It is with the Bible in our hand that we identify our point of departure to be God, the Deity revealed to us in Scripture. We take Him to be our starting point because it could be unquestionably stated that, according to Scripture, atonement is the exclusive work of God through Christ on behalf of sinful human beings. Instead of starting with the sinful state of human beings—with our need for atonement—we commence with a God who voluntarily decided to provide the salvation we needed before we even felt any need for it. Our understanding of God will influence in a direct way a significant number of ideas and conclusions that we will reach concerning the nature of the atonement. I will share with you some of the fundamental aspects of the nature of God that will shape our grasp of the atonement. Obviously what the Bible teaches about the atonement will also affect our understanding of God.

God: A Plurality of Persons

The Christian concept of God is unique, and we should take that uniqueness with us as we study the mystery of the atonement. Scripture clearly declares the existence of only one God while at the same time indicating a plurality of divine persons within the Godhead. Christians have traditionally referred to this teaching as the doctrine of the Trinity. There are not three gods but one God in three persons. We find clear pointers of this teaching in the Old Testament, but it is particularly evident in the New Testament. In fact, it was the outworking of the plan of salvation in the ministry and work of Christ that revealed in an especial way a divine plurality of persons within the Godhead. Christ Himself was the Son of God, the Word of God in human flesh. The Father sent Him, and at a particular moment Christ asked the Father to dispatch to His disciples the Other Comforter, the Holy Spirit. The three of Them worked together for the salvation of the human race. The first demonstration of this mystery took place at the very beginning of the ministry of Christ when during His baptism the three divine Persons had communion with each other (Matt. 3:16, 17).

God as three persons. We should not limit our understanding of God as one and yet a plurality just to the way He operates in the plan of salvation, but should also view it as the mystery of His own person. In other words, the inter-Trinitarian relationship that we witness in God's work of salvation reveals to some extent the eternal inter-Trinitarian relationships within the Godhead. God is in Himself the mystery of the union of three persons. Therefore He is by His very nature a relational being. This is of fundamental importance in the doctrine of the atonement. The atonement is about relationships. It is in fact about the restoration of permanently broken relationships. As a result it reveals a God who is willing to do the unimaginable in order to restore a sector of His creation back to fellowship with Him: "That they may all be one; even as You, Father, are in Me and I in You, that they also may be in Us" (John 17:21, NASB).

God is characterized by pathos. The word "pathos" means that He is a deity of passion and emotions, what we would expect of a relational being. Early in the history of the Christian church the Greek idea of the gods as being so perfect that they were beyond emotion and feeling entered the theology of the church. Since the Greek gods could not experience change, they could not possess emotions at all, because emotions almost by definition imply change. Therefore the gods were detached, indifferent, unchangeable, and unable to be relational in the biblical sense. They were *impassive*. The biblical teaching of the triune God reveals a God who interacts and therefore experiences pathos. He can identify Himself with not only our joys and happiness but also our suffering and pain. He said to Moses, "I have indeed seen the misery of my people in Egypt. I have heard them crying out because of their slave drivers, and I am concerned about their suffering" (Ex. 3:7). The doctrine of the atonement clearly reveals a God who is not detached, but one who descends to our plane in order to participate in our wretchedness and even to take it upon Himself. Without an inter-Trinitarian relationship within God there would hardly be any room left in the Godhead for an atoning sacrifice.

God is one. Although God is three persons, He is still one. It is beyond our rational capabilities to try to understand God in Himself—how He can be one in the mystery of the inter-Trinitarian relationships. However, we can affirm that because God is one, the Godhead possesses a unity of will, purpose, disposition, and action. There are no tensions within the Godhead. Since the atonement is the work of God for us, we have to postulate that the three divine persons were personally involved in it in an expression of one will, purpose, disposition, and action. We should not develop a biblical doctrine of the atonement that would include elements of vindictiveness on the part of one or two members of the Godhead toward another of Them. God cannot hate Himself!

God became flesh. The plurality of persons in the Godhead allows us to distinguish the role of the Son in the atonement from that of the Father and of the Spirit. They are all involved, but each one has a particular function or role. The Son left the eternal glory that He enjoyed with the other members of the Godhead and became flesh (John 1:14). Only God could give us life. The Son was divine, and consequently He had and will ever have life in Himself. In the atonement He gave us life out of Himself. That life did not derive from any other source; otherwise, it would not have been His and He could not have given it to us. In Him was life.

God Is Love

The God of the Scripture is described as being love (1 John 4:8, 16). We employ the word "love" so casually that it is difficult to understand what it means when we apply it to God or when we read that "God is love." But despite that, God uses human experience and language to tell us something about Himself. Even then, we can say only that by appropriating the human parallel God is telling us that His love is similar and yet different from ours. On the one hand, His love reflects the human love of a mother for her child, the love of a wife or husband for the spouse, etc. But on the other hand, it has to be different, not simply because we are finite creatures, but particularly because the corrupting presence of sin and evil in our very existence has distorted our love. Consequently the love of God often surprises us in several unique ways.

Love and the divine action. God's love constantly characterizes and determines His activities. Human love, however, is fundamentally warped by selfish concerns. When we read that God is love, we are dealing not with a philosophical concept but with the dynamic character of our God. Since His nature is love, whatever He does is always and eternally an expression or manifestation of that love. In His interaction with His creatures He is who He is. John, after stating that God is love, adds: "This is how God showed his love among us: He sent his one and only Son into the world that we might live through him" (1 John 4:9). The passage presupposes that love belongs to the very essence of God. By saying, "This is how God showed his love," John indicates that love preceded its specific expression and that the divine act is a revelation of what exists at the very core of the Godhead.[1] There is no duplicity in God, and this makes His love different from ours. While we do not always express love through our actions, that is *never* the case with God.

Love reaches out to the other. God's love is interested in the well-being of the other to the point of a supreme self-sacrifice. Here we can establish an unquestionable direct connection between divine love and the atonement. John comments, in the context of His statement that God is love: "This is love: not that we loved God, but that he loved us and sent his Son as an atoning sacrifice for our sins" (verse 10). Here we have an extremely important theological statement. The text describes divine love as self-sacrificial. God—the Godhead—loved us, and that love revealed itself in the act of Him sending His Son to be our atoning sacrifice. The use of sacrificial language immediately points to the self-giving of God in His Son for the total and absolute benefit of His creatures, particularly those tainted by sin. Here the atonement is grounded and finds its launching board in the very nature of Deity, defined by John as love. We could read that theological statement to mean that the atonement presupposes divine love and not necessarily divine wrath. Yes, the biblical text does speak about divine wrath, but we should not interpret it as in competition with or as essentially different from God's love. Thus we should frame our understanding of the atonement within the biblical perspective of God as love.

Love's object: undeserving human beings. When John declares, "This is love: not that we loved God, but that he loved us," he is implying that God loved us while we still were not only in a state of rebellion against Him but even unable to respond to His love. If we are now able to love, it is "because he first loved us" (verse 19). Our pretended value or lack of it does not determine whether God will love us or not. He has always loved us. Therefore we could say that God's love is indifferent to our value because He loved us in our valueless condition. Paul summarizes this most surprising dimension of divine love when commenting, "When we were still powerless, Christ died for the ungodly. . . . While we were still sinners, Christ died for us" (Rom. 5:7, 8). The divine indifference to the value of the objects of His love points to the freedom of His love. Nothing can manipulate or circumscribe it, because it exceeds anyone's

16

powers or expectations and because it is inseparable from the freedom of the divine being. Above all, His love reaches sinners. We usually refer to this aspect of God's love as His *grace*. Grace is the saving power of the love of God reaching out to undeserving sinful creatures.[2] The mystery of the atonement centers in the fact that it is a divine act of grace that flows out of the very nature of a God who is love. We should never divorce Christ's atoning death from the eternal love of God.

Love restores value. The power of God's love is such that it is able to restore value to repentant sinners. Through the Spirit God pours divine love into the heart of those who find in Christ their Savior and who by faith abide in God and God in them (Rom. 5:5; 1 John 4:13). Our ultimate value resides in our union with God as restored to us through the manifestation of the love of God in Christ. In other words, love makes us valuable in that it unites us to God, the most valuable person in the universe. It is the goal of the atonement to achieve that ultimate act of reunion at a cosmic level.

God Is Holy

The holiness of God points in a special way to His nature as contrasted with creation. Creation is the first divine activity revealed to us and without which we could hardly say anything meaningful about God. In fact, according to Scripture the very first thing we know about God is that He is the Creator (Gen. 1:1). From this fundamental biblical truth all other biblical truth flows in a harmonious and coherent way. It all began at the moment God created free creatures. And it is within the framework of the biblical doctrine of creation and the intromission of the anomaly of evil that we can also speak about the need for, and God's provision of, the atonement. Who is this God who created? He is the holy one. We will discuss several important ideas expressed by that fundamental understanding of God.

God's holiness points to His uniqueness. God's holiness distinguishes Him from the created universe and consequently points to His uniqueness. The Hebrew word *qodesh* ("holy"), when applied to God, "implies a *qualitative* distinction between the divine on the one hand, and human beings and the world on the other."[3] Scripture associates the title "the Holy One of Israel" with God's work of creation in order to emphasize the uniqueness of the Lord and His freedom (Isa. 45:9-12). Since He is the Creator, He is in fact incomparable in that everything else is essentially different from Him. He asked, "'To whom will you compare me? Or who is my equal?' says the Holy One. Lift up you eyes and look to the heavens: Who created all these?" (Isa. 40:25). Here God employed rhetorical questions that demand a negative answer: "There is no one like You!" Hosea stresses the fact that the divine holiness sets God apart from any human being—"'For I am God, and not man'—the holy one among you" (Hosea 11:9).

Even the so-called gods are no match for Him: "Who among the gods is like you, O Lord? Who is like you—majestic in holiness, awesome in glory, working wonders?" (Ex. 15:11; cf. Isa. 46:5-7). "I am God, and there is no other; I am God, and there is none like me" (Isa. 46:9). We should never confuse the Creator with the creature. He is the superlative and supreme expression of holiness: "Holy, holy, holy is the Lord Almighty; the whole earth is full of his glory" (Isa. 6:3). This triadic expression is obviously emphatic and is a Hebrew idiom employed to express the superlative. He is indeed unparalleled in the universe, because He is God. He is the one "who lives forever, whose name is holy" (Isa. 57:15). The atonement is grounded in the uniqueness of a God whose existence is infinitely different from that of the creature.

God's holiness points to His nearness. God's holiness makes room for His closeness to His creatures. He who is holy says, "I live in a high and holy place, but also with him who is contrite and lowly in spirit" (verse 15). Our unique God has chosen to be "the Holy One *of Israel*" (Isa. 55:5). Thus He is both the God who is distant by nature and in His essence and the God who is very close to us. His closeness places His holiness at the service of His people who are at times threatened by the forces of chaos and evil. In His holiness He approaches us "to revive the spirit of the lowly and to revive the heart of the contrite" (Isa. 57:15). The Holy One is the king of all the earth, who dwells in His holy temple (Ps. 47:7, 8), and who also protects His people (Ps. 89:18). It is the Holy One who through His majestic presence and sublime acts saves and redeems His people from the oppression of the enemy: "For I am the Lord, your God, the Holy One of Israel, your Savior" (Isa. 43:3); "your Redeemer, the Holy One of Israel" (verse 14). His uniqueness makes Him invincible.

His love compels Him to be as close as possible to His people, and reached its most sublime expression in the incarnation of the Son of God. He became Immanuel—God with us (Matt. 1:23). In fact, the angel informed Mary that in the mystery of the Incarnation "the holy one to be born will be called the Son of God" (Luke 1:35). We find here an implicit reference to the Holy One of Israel who has now so approached us as to become fully human. The purpose of that closeness to us is to enthrone Him as eternal king over Israel (verses 32, 33) and to "save his people from their sins" (Matt. 1:21). The doctrine of the atonement seeks to explore how the incarnation of the holy Son of God saves us.

God's holiness points to ethical concerns. The holiness of God reveals the moral and ethical concerns of the Godhead. Confronted by divine holiness, Isaiah's awareness of his sinfulness surfaced with a threatening power, and he exclaimed, "Woe to me!" "I am ruined! For I am a man of unclean lips" (Isa. 6:5). He primarily had in mind his moral uncleanness, his sin and guilt, and his need for atonement (verse 7). The uniqueness of God not only involves the fact that we are creatures and that He is the Creator, but also includes the unbridgeable distance between a holy God and sinful creatures. When the Holy One approaches us to sanctify us, this sanctification includes ethical and moral regeneration. The divine call is "Be holy because I, the Lord your God, am holy" (Lev. 19:2). In Israel this included ritual as well as moral purity. He sanctified a particular time (the Sabbath) and a particular place (the holy tabernacle and Temple) to share His holiness with His people and to have fellowship with them.

The fact that God's holiness is incompatible with sin makes it impossible for sinful human beings to relate to it by themselves. The Lord reacts to the presence of sin within the world He created. The prophet says that His "eyes are too pure to look on evil" and that He "cannot tolerate wrong" (Hab. 1:13). He is responsible for preserving and restoring the cosmic order that He established at the beginning. As indicated, His holy presence brings salvation to His people, but it also becomes a life-threatening experience to those who persist in sin and evil. The latter group consists of those who "have forsaken the Lord; they have spurned the Holy One of Israel and turned their backs on him" (Isa. 1:4). His holiness expresses itself in acts of judgment (Isa. 5:24, 25; 10:16-19). But the ultimate purpose of that manifestation of holiness is salvation (Isa. 52:10). A doctrine of the atonement should explore how that holy God is able to save humans in spite of their sinful state.

Conclusion

We begin the study of the atonement with the biblical understanding of God. Our God is unique. The fact that He is a triune deity in Himself will be of great significance in understanding the atonement. Recognizing that He is in His very nature love places the reason for saving sinners in a divine decision free from selfish concerns. God's holiness distinguishes Him from His creatures and explains His reaction against evil and sin. But the fact that He is holy does not mean that He is so absolutely different that we cannot approach Him. The holiness of God manifests itself in His coming near to His intelligent creatures to sanctify them. He dwells with them. It was this wonderful God who, before the creation of the world, determined to sacrifice Himself for the salvation of sinful creatures.

---

[1] Geoffrey Grogan comments along similar lines, observing, "The activity of God is said to be God showing his love. What is shown in fact exists before it is shown. So love must be a quality in the character, the nature of God, which is then revealed in God's loving deeds, and especially in the atoning work of Christ" ("A Biblical Theology of the Love of God," in *Nothing Greater, Nothing Better: Theological Essays on the Love of God*, ed. Kevin J. Vanhoozer [Grand Rapids: Eerdmans, 2001], p. 65).

[2] D. Guthrie and R. P. Martin write concerning the concept of grace in Paul, "The whole concept of grace lies at the heart of Paul's soteriology and in that connection we note that 'the grace of God' denotes an essential feature of God's love. When applied to God, the word grace denotes the favor of God toward those who do not deserve his favor, and therefore came to be used particularly of God's saving work in Christ. It has become a basic assumption, so much so that it frequently occurs in the opening salutations and in the concluding benedictions of the Pauline letters. God is seen as one who bestows unmerited favor on the objects of his love. God's grace is more than his gracious acts, although it includes these. It involves his nature. His love is of such a quality that it gives unstintingly. Grace is another name for the outgoing character of his love, especially to sinners and to his elect people" (D. Guthrie and R. P. Martin, "God," in *Dictionary of Paul and His Letters*, eds. Gerald F. Hawthorne and Ralph P. Martin [Downers Grove, Ill.: InterVarsity, 1993], p. 364). We should not view this as if sin activates divine grace, but rather that covenant breaking "provides the occasion for its demonstration" (Michael S. Horton, *Lord and Servant: A Covenant Christology* [Louisville: Westminster John Knox, 2005], p. 60).

[3] W. Konrfeld, "*Qdš*: I. 1. Etymology," in *Theological Dictionary of the Old Testament*, eds. G. Johannes Botterweck, Helmer Ringgren, and Heinz-Josef Fabry (Grand Rapids: Eerdmans, 2003), vol. 12, p. 522.

2

COSMIC DISTURBANCE:
The Origin of Sin and Evil

The biblical witness is clear: Everything God created was good. This fact transforms the existence of evil and sin in the universe into one of the most difficult topics that theology has to deal with. Much Christian theology has traditionally approached the origin of sin from the perspective of freedom, arguing that a true relationship requires the freedom of all those involved in it. In that case, and from the divine perspective, the fundamental question would appear to have been, Should We create intelligent creatures with free will or irrational beings lacking self-determination? A meaningful creation in which love would freely rule would require the presence of creatures endowed with true liberty.

Freedom, Sin, Evil, and Responsibility

The connection between freedom and responsibility is important when considering the origin of sin and evil. If God created free intelligent creatures, is He not responsible in some way for the phenomenon of sin? If He is, then, the atonement would be grounded, not in sacrificial love, but in the divine need to resolve a problem that He Himself created. To address this concern, we must begin with the conviction that the intelligent creatures God brought into existence were good. Since only some of them developed evil desires while others remained loyal to the Creator, we should conclude that evil was not inevitable but that it was directly related to the use of the will.[1] The distinction between nature and will is of great value in seeking an answer to our question. We could say that the nature of His creatures, as originally created by God, was good, but that their use of their will led to sin and evil. In that case, God is responsible for the first but not for the second. The misuse of the will is based on, but not determined by, the freedom with which God invested His intelligent creatures.[2]

Consequently, Scripture rules out the option that evil and sin originated in God. In fact, with respect to sin's distortion of the universe, it does not assign any level of responsibility to God. The biblical text attributes this most disturbing phenomenon to a heavenly being that rebelled against God. Two prophetic passages particularly speak to the issue. One appears in a judgment speech against the king of Babylon (Isa. 14:12-15) and the other in a similar speech against the king of Tyre (Eze. 28:11-18). Both employ the language and images of the original rebellion in heaven to describe the deep level of corruption of those earthly powers and their ultimate collapse. We will examine those passages and several others.

Origin and Nature of the Cherub

One of the most important pieces of information concerning the originator of evil identifies him as a *cherub* (Eze. 28:14, 16). A cherub is a heavenly angelic being at the service of God, an identification that helps us to understand his nature and his role.

He was a creature. Heavenly beings are neither divine nor self-existent but belong to God's creation. There was a "day" when the cherub was created (verse 15). Ezekiel uses the verb *bārā'* ("to create") to describe his origin. It is the same verb employed in Genesis 1:1. In the Old Testament *bārā'* "is used to express clearly the incomparability of the creative work of God in contrast to all secondary products and likenesses made from already-existing materials by man."[3]

The fact that this angelic being was a creature is important in any discussion about the origin of evil and sin. It first clearly establishes that God is not the direct source of those aberrations and that therefore He is not responsible for the presence of sin in the universe. The fact that God endowed the creature with freedom makes him responsible for the way he employed that gift. Second, the fact that he is a creature indicates that evil and sin are not eternal, coexisting as a parallel force with God. The biblical text rules out any dualistic understanding of evil and sin. Third, being a creature means that the cherub was not self-existent and that, therefore, he will finally come to an end. It suggests that evil and sin will also cease.

He was close to God. A cherub was a type of angel particularly intimate with God. Scripture occasionally associates them with the divine throne, as is the case with the divine throne-chariot in Ezekiel 10:1. A reading of Ezekiel 1 and 10 indicates that "God's throne was movable; it had wheels and was drawn by living creatures (Ezk. 1) referred to in Ezekiel 10 (vv. 15, 20) as *k^erûbîm* [cherubs]."[4] The language is highly symbolic. The prophet depicts the "living creatures" (Eze. 1:15) as having the *likeness* of animals but with the general aspects of a human (verses 5-7). The Bible does not describe their real appearance. The book of Ezekiel symbolically represents them as having four faces—one like an ox, the others like a lion, an eagle, and a man (verse 10)—probably indicating the transcendence of the beings.[5]

John gives a slightly different description of the same beings, though he also places them close to the throne of God in the heavenly temple (Rev. 4:6-8). This association of the cherubs with God's dwelling had its counterpart in the earthly tabernacle in the figures of cherubs embroidered on the veil of the sanctuary and on its inner cover (Ex. 26:1, 31). Solomon adorned the doors of the Temple with carvings of cherubs (1 Kings 6:29-35). Scripture also communicates the connection between the throne of God and the cherubs through the two figures of cherubs placed on the ark of the covenant. In this case they seemed to have had only one face (Ex. 25:17-22). The Old Testament commonly associates the ark of the covenant with the divine throne. It may be perhaps better to say that it functioned as the footstool of God's throne (1 Sam. 4:4; 1 Chron. 28:2; Ps. 132:7).[6]

He was a guardian cherub. With respect to the cherub in Ezekiel, the text states that he was a "covering cherub." Translators sometimes render the phrase as "a guardian [*sākak*] cherub" (Eze. 28:14, 16). But in this case the Hebrew verb means not "to guard" but "to cover, to protect, to veil." The verb also appears in conjunction with the cherubs on the ark of the covenant. Their wings spread upward, "overshadowing [*sākak*] the cover [of the ark] with them," while they looked toward the cover (Ex. 25:20; 37:9). The context does not demand the idea of protection, because the cherubs themselves are rather in an attitude of worship, reverently looking down to the place of atonement and perhaps wondering at the mystery of divine justice and mercy (cf. 1 Peter 1:12). Their wings seem to form a canopy within which God revealed Himself to Moses (cf. Ex. 25:22). Solomon by divine instruction made two large cherubs of wood overlaid with gold and placed between them the ark of the covenant itself: "The cherubim spread their wings over the place of the ark and overshadowed [*sākak*] the ark and its carrying poles" (1 Kings 8:7; cf. 1 Chron. 28:18). Scripture says nothing about the function of the two cherubs. The outstretched wings formed a canopy over the ark of the covenant, perhaps indicating that it was above it that God's invisible throne was located.[7] In that case they would be associated with God's kingship and sovereignty—His universal governance. There is no need to postulate that the covering had a protective significance. With respect to the cherub mentioned in Ezekiel, the text employs the verb *sākak* in the absolute, that is to say, the text does not state what he was covering. In fact, the verb is a participle accompanied by a definite article: "Anointed cherub, *the covering one.*" The reference is to a particular cherub who had a covering function. The cherubs associated with the ark of the covenant provide the best parallel only in the sense that those passages clearly indicate that the cherubs were placed close to the throne of God as coparticipants in the administration of the reign of God and as instruments in the communication of His will. This suggests that this particular cherub had a place of honor in heaven, standing in the light of God's presence and functioning as a vehicle for revealing God's purpose to others.[8] Because it was a position of honor granted to him by the Lord, it would be proper to conclude that "Lucifer was the covering cherub, the most exalted of the heavenly created beings; he stood nearest the throne of God, and was most closely connected and identified with the administration of God's government, most richly endowed with the glory of His majesty and power."[9]

He was influential. As already noted, God assigned this particular cherub a position of honor. The text says: "You were anointed as a guardian cherub, for so I ordained you" (Eze. 28:14). The second line explains the verb "to anoint" with the phrase "I ordained you." The verb *nāthan* ("ordained") expresses here the idea of appointing someone to a position. In this case it increased the celestial being's influence. The text adds: "You walked [*hālak*] among the fiery stones" (verse 14). The verb *hālak* means "to go to and fro, to walk about," and expresses "his freedom and especially his supervisory role"[10] (see Job 1:7). The cherub freely moved about, observing what was happening around him. Such type of walk is purposefully oriented (Gen. 13:17). He freely traveled "on the holy mount of God" (Eze. 28:14), previously referred to as "the garden of God," Eden (verse 13). The "mount of God" is the location of His heavenly dwelling and where the heavenly council meets with the Lord. Isaiah refers to it as "the mount of assembly" (Isa. 14:13). By referring to it as the Garden of Eden, the biblical author emphasizes the paradisiacal nature of the heavenly dwelling. The cherub resides in that glorious place, serving the Lord and consequently exercising an important leadership role among the heavenly host.

He was blameless. Scripture describes the "ways" of this heavenly figure, that is to say his conduct, as "blameless" (Eze. 28:15). The appellation applies to both his inner being and the outer expression of it in his personal behavior. The statement seeks to indicate that the being had nothing essentially wrong with him. God had created him in a state of blamelessness, without any defect. The noun *tāmîm* primarily expresses the idea of completeness, undamaged, and without defect, and from that concrete use it developed ethical and religious meanings. Therefore, *tāmîm* is something that is complete, "a totality without a diminution."[11] The ethical, moral, and religious usages of the term derive from the conviction that it is important to preserve the order of life in society, the bonds that hold it together. The sentence "You were blameless in your ways" designates a person who contributes to the preservation of that order. Concerning the Lord Himself, Scripture declares, "As for God, his way is perfect [*tāmîm*]" (2 Sam. 22:31). He who created order in the world does not alter it but preserves it.

The Psalms in a particular way provide a clear picture of the religious and ethical meaning of *tāmîm*. To be blameless is to walk according to the Torah, the divine instruction (Ps. 119:1). The psalmist asked, "Lord, who may dwell in your sanctuary?" And the answer given is "He whose walk is blameless [*tāmîm*]" (Ps. 15:2). The psalmist further explains this as a person who will "do what is right," those who are truthful from their heart, do not slander, do not do any wrong to others, honor and fear the Lord, keep their oaths, and who do not exploit and abuse others for personal benefit (verses 2-4). A blameless way of life honors God and shows respect to others. That kind of life characterized the cherub who dwelled on the mount of the Lord from the moment of his creation.

The Fall of the Cherub

The origin of sin is and will remain forever a mystery beyond the comprehension of any intelligent creature in the universe. But although it escapes our full grasp we can still understand something about it, just as, for instance, we do some aspects of the mystery of the Incarnation. It is simply that sin lacks a reason for existence. At first glance the fact that it came into being at all may give the impression that it might have a purpose. But our discussion about its origin will reveal that it is purposeless and meaningless, and that it robs everything else of its significance. Sin is grounded on a lie.

Wickedness found in him. The mystery of its origin becomes evident in Ezekiel 28:15: "You were blameless in your ways from the day you were created till wickedness [*'awlah*] was found [*mātsa'*] in you." While Scripture clearly explains the blamelessness of the cherub as the product of divine creation, wickedness is an unexpected phenomenon that is simply "found." God did not originally make him that way. Legal contexts often employ the passive form of the verb *mātsa'* ("to find") to indicate that what was found was the result of a judicial process (cf. Esther 2:23; Ps. 17:3; 1 Sam. 25:28).[12] The implication would then be that the strange behavior of the cherub was legally examined and it *was found* to be wicked. What makes the legal examination necessary is precisely that the behavior of the cherub does not correspond to what would be expected of him—he was disrupting God's established order. The judicial process determines that there was in him "wickedness" (*'awlah*).

The noun *'awlah* means "badness, malice, injustice,"[13] and basically designates incorrectness and perversity.[14] The emphasis of the term is less on the specific sinful act and more on the "general negative assessment of a person's behavior and actions."[15] Scripture calls such persons "sons of *'awlah*," that is to say, perversity and injustice has warped their character (e.g., 2 Sam. 3:34; 7:10; Ps. 89:22; 1 Chron. 17:9). More specifically the term refers, first, to that which is incorrect and illegal.[16] Those who commit this type of crime have "departed from the right path, from the legal system to which a person must adhere; they deviated from that system and violated it"[17] (cf. 2 Sam. 3:28-30, 34). One could even argue that "the characteristic feature of such persons is that they do not adhere to the proclaimed will of God,"[18] to His law (e.g., Hosea 10:9). Second, the term expresses the idea of duplicity, that is to say, such persons pretend to be doing the right thing when in reality they do not (e.g., Deut. 25:13-16). Such actions reveal the inner condition of the person in that they require planning and cunningness (cf. Ps. 64:7). Third, ʿawlah communicates the implication of disloyalty. Zephaniah 3:13 sees those with ʿawlah as speaking lies, which in this case refers "not to false accusation but to disloyalty and deception in daily human relations and in one's relationship to Yahweh"[19] (cf. Isa. 59:3; Hosea 7:13). Individuals use such speech against God, placing it at the service of injustice, unrest (e.g., Mal. 2:6), misrepresentation (e.g., Job 13:7) and slander (e.g., Eze. 22:9). Fourth, in some biblical passages ʿawlah designates the people's rejection of the Lord and expresses the idea of apostasy (Jer. 8:5; Ps. 78:36, 37).

We can conclude that the term ʿawlah describes not only a particular illegal deed that upsets the social and moral order by damaging others in different ways, but also the inner disposition of a person to commit the crime.[20] The use of the Hebrew term in the Old Testament suggests that the cherub showed disloyalty to God by acting in a way that significantly upset the heavenly social and legal structure. Elements of duplicity were probably present.

Widespread trade, violence, and sin. Ezekiel portrays the cherub as involved in trade (rᵉkullah) that filled him with violence (úāmās) and resulted in sin (chāʿaʾ) (Eze. 28:16). The text depicts him as a merchant, who, in the context, is trading (spreading or selling) a spirit of rebellion. It suggests that others are listening to him. The root meaning of the term rᵉkullah designates a person who walks about, and from there it was applied to the merchant who journeys from place to place to sell his or her goods—a peddler.[21] The passage in Ezekiel sees the cherub as actively involved in the spread of what he considered to be his goods. The word rᵉkullah is also related to the noun rākîl, which means "slander." If we apply that meaning to this context, then the text would be charging that the cherub was slandering the Lord in many ways, that is to say, speaking badly, falsely, and maliciously against Him. In doing that, he was "filled with violence [úāmās]."

The Old Testament uses the Hebrew noun úāmās, usually translated "violence," primarily in the context of social and legal interaction. Designating an inappropriate way of relating to others that violates their rights, it involves the illegal "appropriation of what belongs to God or one's neighbor" and is "motivated by greed and hate and often making use of physical violence and brutality"[22] (e.g., Zeph. 3:4; Eze. 22:26). Such violence could result in murder (e.g.,

26

Gen. 49:5; Judges 9:24). Or it could be verbal, consisting in the humiliation of the victim "through impudent self-aggrandizement"[23] (Gen. 16:5), by influencing others to do evil (Prov. 10:6), or by falsely accusing someone (Ps. 55:3, 4). In the case of false accusations, hate is its source (e.g., Prov. 10:3; Ps. 27:12).[24]

With respect to the ascription of violence to the cherub, the passage most probably has in mind verbal violence in the form of false accusations, influencing others to do evil, and self-aggrandizement. Notice that it is his many trades/slanders that fill his interior (Heb. *tāwek*, "midst, inside, inner part") with violence. By expressing his negative feelings, he corrupted himself even more and the feelings gave way to a spirit of violence. The cherub was filled with violence—he was infected by it—and became totally corrupted from inside out. Once he reached that stage in his self-corruption the Lord could do nothing but bring judgment against him. Like the inhabitants of the antediluvian world, who were also filled with violence (Gen. 6:11), the cherub had to confront God's judgment against him.

Ezekiel 28:16 employs another term to describe the conduct of the cherub: "You were filled with violence, and *you sinned*." Violence is sin. The Old Testament uses the Hebrew verb *chā‹a‘* ("to sin") to designate sin in its broadest sense as an action that misses God's intended goal for humans, or the human failure to live up to His expectations, and that alienates them from God.[25] "Like other words related to the notion of 'sin' it assumes an absolute standard or law" that is violated.[26] Again we face the fact that the cherub, through his actions and words against God, was upsetting the Lord's established order by not submitting to His law.

"Your heart became proud" (Eze. 28:17). Until now the primary emphasis has been on the external actions of the cherub that revealed the presence of self-corruption. Now we will examine his inner being—his heart. Here we come face to face with the inexplicable nature of sin. Sin is directly related to pride. The verb *gābah* literally means "to be high" (e.g., Job 5:7; 1 Sam. 10:23), and from that concrete meaning it came to indicate both "to be exalted" in a positive way (e.g., Job 36:7), and "to be haughty" (e.g., Isa. 3:16; Eze. 16:50). Pride is a self-perception that consists of seeing oneself as superior to others. It is fundamentally a distorted view of oneself that upsets the social and religious order.[27] Thus it designates people who "inappropriately lift themselves up to exalted positions by claiming power and authority over circumstances that are beyond their control"[28] and to which they do not have a legitimate claim (2 Chron. 26:16).

The cherub became proud and sought to justify his irrational feeling and attitude by grounding it on his "beauty" (Heb. *yᵒpî*) and "splendor" (Heb. *yipᶜah*). The Bible associates beauty with the form of the object, its appearance (Gen. 39:6; 41:18; 1 Sam. 17:42). Beauty also includes the actions and abilities of a person (S. of Sol. 6:10; Prov. 11:22). Ezekiel focuses on the impressive appearance of the cherub that led him to become proud. An obsession with beauty could lead to "arrogant disregard of God"[29] (Isa. 3:16-24; Eze. 27:3-5). "Splendor" refers to the brightness of the cherub, to his appearance. The verbal form of that noun ($yāpa^c$) means "to shine forth, to cause to shine," and it often refers to the manifestation of the Lord (Deut. 33:2-4; Ps. 50:2-6; 94:1-3). When He shows Himself, the light of His presence blazes forth, indicating His majestic power. According to Psalm 80:1, the light of God's presence shines forth from His throne above the cherubim. Since the cherubim are so close to God they seem to participate in His splendor. This condition somehow "corrupted" (shacha‹) the "wisdom" (chakmah) of the cherub.

In the Old Testament wisdom designates the intelligence, skills, and cleverness needed to master life, to preserve it, and to enjoy it, and is characterized by socioreligious concerns. The biblical writers consider wisdom to be a divine gift (1 Kings 5:7, 12; James 1:5) that contributes to the proper social and religious interaction of individuals with each other and with God. In general, Scripture relates wisdom to adherence to the law of God, which the Bible considers as a source of wisdom (Deut. 4:6). Because of his pride, the cherub "corrupted" his wisdom (Eze. 28:17). He became a fool by placing it at the service of his own personal interest. The verb shacha‹ ("to corrupt") means "to ruin, destroy, annihilate." The cherub took what was good and mysteriously ruined it by misusing it. This undoubtedly resulted in disregard for others and in the disruption of social and religious order and peace.

Issues in the Conflict

We have been describing the inner corruption of the cherub as stimulated by his superficial perception of his outward appearance and his unusual wisdom. Through an act of self-deception his feelings of superior beauty and wisdom provided a rationalization for his pride. But the biblical text takes us beyond that self-perception to the inner motivations deep within his heart, helping us at the same time to understand better some of the central issues in the conflict. At its core we find the true intentions of the cherub: "You said in your heart, 'I will ascend to heaven; I will raise my throne above the stars of God; I will sit enthroned on the mount of assembly. . . . I will make myself like the Most High'" (Isa. 14:13, 14; cf. Eze. 28:8).

To be like the Most High. Scripture now interprets the pride of the cherub in terms of his dissatisfaction with the specific role assigned to him by God as one of His creatures. No longer content with his privileged position as a covering cherub, he aspired to more, and consequently developed feelings of inferiority. Apparently he toyed with the idea of crossing the infinite threshold that separated the creature from the Creator. The ultimate goal of his pride became clear: Desiring to be as high/exalted as God was by taking over His role, he sought his own enthronement in the heavenly temple as the cosmic king (or at least sharing the throne with Him—"I will sit enthroned on the mount of the assembly" (Isa. 14:13). It was fundamentally a conflict between this particular cherub and God.

If we were to ask how a perfect creature could venture into that new pattern of thinking, we would be confronted with impenetrable darkness. We could only reaffirm the fact that it is the freedom of the creature that could have led him to explore such improbable channels of thought. At this point one would have to ask about the state of the cherub's rational faculties. Should not his untainted reason alert him to the fact that what he was exploring was totally irrational and obviously beyond the potential of a creature? The process of self-corruption must have involved a significant amount of time during which the emotional side of the cherub took over and brought unbalance and instability to his inner being. He indeed was misusing the freedom that God had granted him by delving into emotions and thoughts that were slowly but certainly leading him down the road of darkness. Evil was mysteriously gestating within his very being.

Decentralization of the self. The texts describing the self-corruption of the cherub make clear that his activities upset God's established order. The divine order centered on the loving will of the Creator toward His creatures. Within the divine system unselfish service to God and others constituted the nucleus of each being's existence—that is to say, it provided for them existential orientation and made their life meaningful within that order. In that original state of affairs the monstrosity of evil expressed itself as the decentralization and disorientation of the self. Evil was a claim for independence from the system of order that nurtured the creature, made possible existence, and that led to self-realization through selfless service. A cherub now sought to be as self-sufficient as God Himself had always been. But it was deeper than that. In contradistinction to God, he was not only claiming self-sufficiency but particularly self-centeredness manifested in pride. The moment that any part of God's good, intelligent creation pulled apart from the rest, it disrupted and damaged cosmic *shalom* (peace).

Opposition to God's expressed will. Closely related to what we just discussed is the rebellion of the cherub against God's law of love. Driven by pride, he rejected the principle of unselfish love that ruled the universe. In its place he promoted self-rule by rejecting God's will for him and for others. John writes: "The devil has been sinning since the beginning" (1 John 3:8). The verse takes us back to the moment that heaven found sin in the cherub. As indicated above, that sin consisted in doing what was illegal or simply departing from the legal system established by God (Heb. ʿawlah, "injustice"—Eze. 28:15). Since then, John says, the devil has been constantly sinning—that is to say, he has been acting in continuous opposition to divine law.

A close connection exists between sin and the law: "Everyone who sins breaks the law; in fact, sin is lawlessness [anomia]" (1 John 3:4). The term anomia is formed by the privative prefix a ("not, without") plus the noun nomos ("law"), and it means "without respect for the law," referring to a "state or condition of being disposed to what is lawless."[30] With respect to humans, whenever anomia "increases, their love for each other decreases (according to Matthew [24:12]); for 'the law and the prophets' are merely the explication of the command to love God and the neighbor (22:34-40)."[31] This same attitude and condition must have characterized the cherub. Anomia replaced the eternal divine law of love. But Christ came "to destroy the devil's work" (1 John 3:8), and those who belong to Him know that they are children of God and not of the devil because they love one another (verse 11). From the beginning the enemy has been promoting lawlessness, while Christ proclaimed the rule of love. The conflict has not yet finished.

The historical and eschatological adversary of Christ—the Antichrist—Paul describes as "the lawless one" (2 Thess. 2:9). The apostle considers this anti-law attitude in agreement with or "in accordance with the work of Satan" (verse 9). This passage is important in that it establishes that Satan's opposition to the law of God at the beginning of the cosmic conflict will be an important issue at its close. His aim as the lawless one will be "the destruction of that all-encompassing order of things revealed in the nomos [law]."[32] It has been his intention from the moment he rebelled against God. We can conclude that in the cosmic conflict, submission to the loving will of God as expressed in His law of love continues to play a significant role.

Attack against God's character and government. An attack against the divine will is almost by definition one against God's character, because the law is a reflection of the divine personality. Ezekiel revealed that the cherub was characterized by slanderous attacks and verbal violence. Such an attitude is inseparable from and is in fact an expression of pride. Pride includes attacks aimed at diminishing or belittling the real value of others—in this case, God. We could use two biblical examples to illustrate how the enemy sought to do this.

Narrative of Genesis 3: The first one appears in Genesis 3 and took place during the conversation between Eve and the serpent. The narrative reveals several things about the rebellious spirit of God's enemy. First, he tried to misrepresent God. He approached Eve and asked her, "Did God really say, 'You must not eat from any tree in the garden'?" (Gen. 3:1). The question insinuated that God did not disclose to them His real intentions for humanity, and that consequently He was unreliable. Second, the serpent openly contradicted God's expressed will for Adam and Eve. He charged that God had lied to them (verse 4). Although God had said that eating from the forbidden tree would result in death, the serpent retorted, "You will not surely die." God had a dark side to Him, the serpent suggested, that humans were ignorant of. Humans, he further argued, were really slaves, unable to achieve their fullness of being through the fear of death inculcated in them by God Himself. Freedom in union to God was an illusion. Self-realization was possible only through self-determination. Third, the serpent revealed his low view of God when he assured the humans that they could be like God. This new understanding of the creature was an expression of his personal pride when in the mountain of the Lord he, as the covering cherub, sought to be like God. The only barrier to that most exalted position, he implied, was the restrictive will of God. But by attempting to exalt the creature, he was bringing God down from His rightfully exalted position as Creator to that of the creature.

Narrative of Job 1 and 2: The second narrative occurs in the book of Job. During the meeting of the heavenly council Satan and God had a discussion about God's faithful servant Job. The Lord characterizes him as a person who "is blameless and upright, a man who fears God and shuns evil" (Job 1:8). The conversation that followed revealed the inner thoughts and feelings of the enemy. First, he tried to establish that humans do not serve God out of unselfish love. Job, Satan claimed, regarded God as a provider, and as long as the Lord met his needs, the human would continue to honor Him. In other words, the relationship between Job and God was based not on love but on self-interest. The claim that it was possible for the creatures to respond and relate to God on the basis of pure love was groundless. Selfishness, not self-sacrificial love, Satan argued, was what ruled the universe. Second, he argued that the true nature of the creature manifests itself in the context of chaos and not within the order established by God. The dissolution of that artificial structure would allow the creature to become self-sufficient by breaking away from the Lord—that is to say, by cursing Him. So Satan asked God to stop being the provider in order for Job to be himself (Job 1:11; 2:5). This, according to him, would demonstrate that the relationship was in essence shaped by selfishness.

Third, and even more important, Satan was in a particular way rejecting the integrity of God's character and His system of governance. He argued that the Lord is by nature a selfish being interested only in the service of His intelligent creatures. According to him, it manifested itself in two interrelated ways. God overprotected them in order to win their loyalty, thus satisfying His own self-interest, while in the process developing and nurturing egocentrism in His creatures. God's selfish nature also revealed itself, Satan added, in the manner that

He ruled the universe. He was constantly giving to them, enriching them, in order to make them dependent on Him. If they did well with what He gave to them, then He would offer them even more to administer for Him. It was through this type of relationship that He gained their service. So the system He used to preserve cosmic unity was anchored in self-centeredness; and it motivated more of the same. What ruled the universe was not selfless love but the principle of self-preservation according to which we attach to each other in order to derive from the other what we need to survive. God, Satan argued, was responsible for this state of affairs, which He tried to conceal by claiming that what holds the cosmos together is self-sacrificial love. If God would only withdraw His protection, ending His role as provider, it would become clear that the relationship between Him and His creatures resulted from self-interest—a mentality that God Himself had been nurturing. Not only were they serious charges against God; they demonstrated the constant attitude and thinking of the fallen angel. The conflict was indeed between him and God.

Expulsion From the Mountain of the Lord

At some point during the conflict of wills in the heavenly dwelling of God a final determination took place with respect to the rebellious angel. The preservation of order required the expulsion of the fallen cherub: "I drove you in disgrace from the mount of God, and I expelled you, O guardian cherub" (Eze. 28:16; Isa. 14:12). The cherub gained the support of a number of angels "who did not keep their positions of authority but abandoned their own home—these he [God] has kept in darkness, bound with everlasting chains for judgment on the great Day" (Jude 6; cf. 2 Peter 2:4). The book of Revelation uses the images of this original conflict in heaven to describe Christ's victory over Satan on the cross and in the process gives us some more information about what occurred in heaven. The purpose of this flashback to the original conflict was to indicate not only that Christ defeated the rebellious angels in heaven, but also that He conquered them again once and for all on the cross: "And war broke out in heaven; Michael and his angels fought against the dragon. The dragon and his angels fought back, but they were defeated, and there was no longer any place for them in heaven. The great dragon was thrown down, that ancient serpent, who is called the Devil and Satan, the deceiver of the whole world—he was thrown down to the earth, and his angels were thrown down with him" (Rev. 12:7-9, NRSV).

The cosmic conflict did not end then—it had just begun. God had decided not to destroy the rebellious angels immediately, but to make room for their freedom to express itself even in a corrupted form. The origin of evil affected the cosmos in ways that we are not aware of and brought with it disorientation. God's intelligent creatures did not know how to relate to the new phenomenon. The question remained, Who is right in this conflict? How would one know? Only a cosmic judgment could clarify the issues.

Conclusion

The Bible assigns the origin of sin to an intelligent heavenly being who mysteriously corrupted himself and rebelled against God. The charges he raised against God came to occupy a central place in the cosmic conflict. The doctrine of the atonement should address in a fully satisfactory way the issue of evil and sin. It should be able, based on the life, work, and ministry of Christ, to answer fully all the questions raised by the rebellious cherub concerning the nature of God, His character, justice, love, and the integrity of His cosmic government and Lordship.

---

[1] Augustine of Hippo (354-430) originally stated the idea as follows: "It is not permissible to us to doubt that the contrasting appetites of the good and the bad angels have arisen not from a difference in their nature and origin—for God, the good Author and Creator of all substances, created them both—but from a difference in their wills and desires" (*The City of God*, 12. 1).

[2] See Gordon Graham, *Evil and Christian Ethics* (New York: Cambridge University Press, 2001), pp. 200, 201.

[3] Karl-Heinz Bernhardt, "*Bārā'*: III. Meaning," in *Theological Dictionary of the Old Testament*, vol. 2, p. 246.

[4] D. N. Freedman and M. P. O'Connor, "*Kerûb*," in *Theological Dictionary of the Old Testament*, vol. 7, p. 312.

[5] It may be useful to point out that even though the selection of these animals may seem to us arbitrary, "they were perfectly natural for Ezekiel's world. Not only do they appear frequently on ancient iconographic and glyptic art; they also had symbolic significance for the Israelites. The lion was renowned for its strength, ferocity, and courage (Judg. 14:18; 2 Sam. 1:23; 17:10), and served as a symbol of royalty. The eagle was the swiftest and most stately of birds (Deut. 28:49; Isa. 40:31; Jer. 48:40). The ox (or 'cattle'—*šôr* does not specify sex) was not only the most valuable domestic animal (Prov. 14:4) but also functioned as a symbol of both fertility and divinity (cf. Ps. 106:19, 20). The human, being created as the image of God and invested with divine majesty (Gen. 1:28; Ps. 8), is the most dignified and noble of all" (Daniel I. Block, *The Book of Ezekiel, Chapters 1-24* [Grand Rapids: Eerdmans, 1997], p. 96).

[6] For more on this topic, consult C. L. Seow, "Ark of the Covenant," in *Anchor Bible Dictionary*, ed. David Noel Freedman (New York: Doubleday, 1992), vol. 1, pp. 386-393).

[7] As suggested above, neither the cherubs nor the ark of the covenant should be identified with God's throne. The phrase "who is enthroned between the cherubim" (1 Sam. 4:4) is sometimes taken to mean that the cherubs form the throne of God. But the Hebrew text does not have the preposition "between." It is "entirely possible that the epithet is intended to evoke the picture of YHWH, surrounded by cherubim, seated upon his throne (cf. 1 Kgs. 22:19; Isa. 6:1f.)" (Cornelis Houtman, *Historical Commentary on the Old Testament: Exodus* [Leuven: Peeters, 2000], vol. 3, p. 384).

[8] See, Ellen G. White, *The Desire of Ages* (Mountain View, Calif.: Pacific Press, 1898), p. 758.

33

[9] Ellen G. White, "The Words and Works of Satan Repeated in the World," *Signs of the Times*, Apr. 28, 1890.

[10] Block, *The Book of Ezekiel, Chapters 25-48*, p. 114.

[11] B. Kedar-Kopfstein, "*Tām*," in *Theological Dictionary of the Old Testament*, vol. 15, p. 702.

[12] S. Wagner and H.-J. Fabry, "*Mātsa`*," in *Theological Dictionary of the Old Testament*, vol. 8, pp. 474, 475.

[13] Ludwig Koehler, Walter Baumgartner, and Johann Jakob Stamm, *Hebrew and Aramaic Lexicon of the Old Testament* (Leiden: Brill, 2001), vol. 1, p. 798).

[14] R. Knierim, *`Awel, Perversity*," in *Theological Lexicon of the Old Testament*, eds. Ernst Jenni and Claus Westermann (Peabody, Mass.: Hendrickson, 1997), vol. 2, p. 849.

[15] J. Schreiner, "*`Awlah*," in *Theological Dictionary of the Old Testament*, vol. 10, p. 524.

[16] Knierim, "*`Awel, Perversity*," in *Theological Lexicon of the Old Testament*, vol. 2, p. 850.

[17] Schreiner, "*`Awlah*," p. 524.

[18] *Ibid.*

[19] *Ibid.*, p. 526.

[20] *Ibid.*, p. 527.

[21] cf. E. Lipinski, "*Rkl*," *Theological Dictionary of the Old Testament*, vol. 13, p. 498.

[22] *Ibid.*, p. 479.

[23] *Ibid.*, p. 482.

[24] *Ibid.*

[25] Cf. Herbert G. Livingston, "*Chā`a`*," in *Theological Word Book of the Old Testament*, eds. R. L. Harris, G. L. Archer, Jr., and B. K. Waltke (Chicago: Moody, 1980), vol. 1, pp. 277, 278; and Alex Luc, "*Chā`a`*," in *New International Dictionary of the Old Testament Theology and Exegesis*, ed. Willem A. VanGemeren (Grand Rapids: Zondervan, 1997), vol. 2, p. 89.

[26] Livingston, "*Chā`a`*," p. 278.

[27] R. Hentschke, "*Gābhah*," in *Theological Dictionary of the Old Testament*, vol. 2, p. 359, states, "*Gbh* is used to characterize the aspirations and relationships of men with God and with their fellow men in a religiously and ethically negative sense (Prov. 16:5 in particular is severe when it says that everyone that is proud of heart is a *to`abhath yhvh*, 'an abomination to Yahweh'), and thus should be translated 'haughty, proud, presumptuous,' etc."

[28] Gary V. Smith and Victor P. Hamilton, "*Gbh*," in *New International Dictionary of Old Testament Theology Exegesis*, vol. 1, p. 797.

[29] Helmer Ringgren, "*Yāpah*," in *Theological Dictionary of the Old Testament*, vol. 6, p. 219.

[30] Frederick W. Danker, *Greek-English Lexicon of the New Testament and Other Early Christian Literature* (Chicago: University of Chicago Press), p. 85.

[31] M. Limbeck, "*Anomia*, Lawlessness, Breaking of the Law," in *Exegetical Dictionary of the New Testament*, eds. Horst Robert Balz and Gerhard Schneider (Grand Rapids: Eerdmans, 1990-1993), vol. 1, p. 107.

[32] *Ibid.*

3

A RACE IS
Fallen

The question of the origin of life on our planet continues to be a matter of debate among the specialists who so far have not been able to agree on a common answer. But more intriguing is the question of the origin of human (self-conscious) life on our world. The biblical answer is in many ways simple and at the same time deep and mysterious. We find our origin in the musings of the divine mind—we began as a thought of God. At some point in God's eternity He determined to create humans in His own image, a new race in the cosmos. Leaving nothing to chance, God planned every aspect of those complex creatures. He was going to prepare the proper physical environment for them, a beautiful planet with a flora characterized by a wonderful diversity of color and expression and a fauna rich in different forms of life. Then He would place humans there. The cosmic equilibrium created by the Lord made possible the existence of a multiplicity of life forms as well as that of intelligent life.

Untainted Humans

The biblical text seeks not to solve the mystery of the existence of humans but rather to deepen it by directly connecting their origin to God. That God created us means that we are not an accident—that we are not just the end product of mindless natural law. We are the result of divine reflection, analysis, and the expression of divine freedom, power, and love. Such divine intentionality places a high value on the human race and indissolubly binds us to God in a Creator-creature relationship. At its deepest level creation in the image of God means precisely that we can have fellowship with Him.

Fellowship with God. As already indicated, the plurality of persons within the Godhead unveils the fact that God is social and that consequently fellowship is part of His essence. Being created in the image of God defines humans as social beings existing in fellowship with others. The first social relationship that

Adam established was with God. The Creator breathed the breath of life into his nostrils, and the first man became a living being. This was life, but not divine life, as if Adam were now participating in the very life of God. Rather it was created life. When Adam opened his eyes, his brain registered its first image, that of God. Two persons looked at each other in the Garden of Eden, and as a result they were bound to each other in the most glorious fellowship that humans could ever have.

Also Eve's first social interaction was not with Adam, but with God. He intentionally planned it that way. The Creator put Adam to sleep not because He did not want Adam to feel pain during the "surgery," but in order for Eve to enjoy the same privilege he had, namely to experience fellowship with God before having it with Adam. The enjoyment of union with God defined humans as unique, setting them apart from the rest of the created world. They found their greatest joy in life in an existence characterized by unhindered fellowship with the Lord.

Fellowship with other humans. The primary relationship of humans, and the one that would determine the possibility and quality of any other relationship, involved their union with God. After establishing that grounding relationship, the Lord brought Adam and Eve together. Doing so established a new multifaceted type of relationship. It consisted not only of a relationship between two human beings, but also one between husband and wife, and between a plurality of persons (God and humans). God immediately promised them, in the form of a blessing, that their social circle would increase as they multiplied themselves through procreation (Gen. 1:28). The Creator intended that they should maintain such a union of love forever in the beautiful and peaceful setting that He had prepared for their enjoyment.

Interaction with nature. The setting in which God placed humans required them to interface with it. Characterized by perfect ecological balance, its perfection contributed to human happiness. As the image of God, humans, male and female, were to represent the government of God in the sphere of the natural world. In a sense it could be said that with respect to the rest of creation, they were to be God's coregents. The Creator said to them: "Rule over the fish of the sea and the birds of the air, over the livestock, over all the earth, and over all the creatures that move along the ground" (verse 26). The Old Testament employs the verb "to rule" (Heb. *rādah*) to refer to the authority of the king (e.g., Ps. 72:8; 110:2; Isa. 41:2). Its use in Genesis implies that while royal dominion was entrusted to Adam and Eve, it was not absolute. Since they were coregents with God, the natural world did not belong to them. The Lord immediately set limits to that power by establishing that they will eat only seed-bearing plants and from "every tree that has fruit with seed in it" (Gen. 1:29). They had no right to take the life of animals to preserve theirs. Rather, they were to exercise their power within a creation that was "very good" (verse 31). In addition, they were also part of that same creation. Their dominion presupposed an edenic setting in which its wholeness remained intact.

Freedom of will and action. When God created humans, He endowed them with freedom, a fact revealed in the narrative in several ways. First, fellowship presupposes freedom. Union with God does not take place outside the realm of human history—that is, in some mystical sphere that erases self-consciousness. Instead, union with God is fellowship with Him in our mode of existence as creatures, and it presupposes willingness on the part of humans to participate in it. Otherwise there is no freedom. Second, fellowship with other humans also presupposes that same type of freedom by which we not only interact with them but also accept and love them. Third, the capacity to rule, to be a coregent, requires freedom to think and act—otherwise humans could not satisfactorily accomplish their responsibility. Finally, the intellectual dimension of human nature needs to be exercised in the context of freedom of thinking. This capacity to think and analyze appears in the biblical narrative when the Creator asked Adam to give names to all animals (Gen. 2:19). The task indicated not only that they were under the dominion of Adam, but also that he needed to study their behavior in order for the name to correspond to the nature of the animal. It involved freedom of thinking and speech.

Possibly the most important passage supporting the fact that God created humans free is Genesis 2:16, 17: "You are free to eat from any tree in the garden; but you must not eat from the tree of the knowledge of good and evil, for when you eat of it you will surely die." Eating is an instinctive response to a build-in need in our being that does not require freedom. Even telling humans what to eat is not necessarily an endowment of freedom. The idea of freedom surfaces in all its power and beauty when God commands them not to eat from a certain tree. The command itself was meaningful only in the context of the freedom of individuals to obey or not to obey it. Otherwise, why would it be necessary to give a command? Why not make abstention from eating from that particular tree an instinctive response, a mechanical action?

But what kind of freedom gives you only the option to choose death? Could not the threat of death become an enslaving power that would deprive humans of freedom to act? In order to explore the true implications of those questions, we need to approach them from the angle of the choices available to humans. It is difficult to think of a created being as a free agent. For obvious reasons God brought Adam and Eve into existence without their free consent. God *in His freedom* and sovereignty decided and proceeded to create them. Their freedom emerged after their creation in the form of the possibility of a choice. The choices at the disposal of Adam and Eve were not many—they had only two.

We find both of the choices that they confronted in the text we quoted above. A superficial reading may give the impression that the choices were either to eat or not to eat from the tree. But they were not really about eating, although it did involve that. The narrative takes us to the very depth of the nature of human freedom and establishes that such freedom has to do with the most fundamental question a creature has to address—that of choosing life or death. The biblical writer is not telling us that the universe possesses two eternal antagonistic forces, namely the power of God as life and the power of someone or something else as death, and that we can select between them. The issues are much more complex.

Let me suggest for your consideration that what the text establishes is that only God *is,* and that apart from Him there is nothing else. The choice is not between God and something else, but between being with God and not being. This makes absolute sense within the flow of the narrative. As already indicated, Adam and Eve came into being without giving them freedom to choose to be created or not. That was a logical impossibility. But now the Creator did offer them the freedom to choose existence or nonexistence, that is to say, to freely accept the gift of life or to go back to nothingness. God offered the options in the form of a firm command, because the Creator had a preference. He wanted them to select life, and therefore He emphasized as strongly as possible that if they opted for death He would honor their choice and that they would "surely die."

Obviously, rejecting God's gift of life would be to spurn Him, an act of rebellion, but He was willing to accept their decision. Since God's intention for humans was positive, it is difficult to imagine that Adam and Eve would have seriously considered the possibility of rejecting life. But the option was there—otherwise God would have enslaved them to live on our planet for ever and ever without their consent. This brings us to the serpent.

The Human Fall Into Sin

The Fall of Adam and Eve resulted from Satan's deceitful interpretation of the divine command we just discussed. Having said that, I should point out that when it comes to sin against God, humans have no excuse. What is surprising is that in the Garden of Eden the evil one used one of God's good creatures to achieve his destructive purposes. It suggests that the cosmic conflict has rules of engagement. God allowed the tempter to have access to the couple, but their Creator was free to alert them about the intention of the fallen angel and to urge them to be watchful. The rest would be determined by the way the humans would use their freedom, one that made them accountable for their actions.[1]

The command provided for the enemy an opportunity to engage Eve in a dialogue and to evaluate God's intentions toward humans. He tempted her to explore new possibilities for self-realization by misusing her freedom. As we mentioned above, the enemy ascribed to God evil intentions by presenting the command as a restriction of their development instead of an affirmation of human freedom. He offered Eve a new possibility. God had said to the couple that they had the freedom to accept or reject life—that was true freedom. Now the enemy offered to the woman a third option: absolute autonomy. According to the enemy, this type of existence did not depend on anyone else and transcended the possibility of death. He was offering her the divine mode of existence: "You will be like God, knowing good and evil" (Gen. 3:5). The serpent invited Eve to reject her childlike dependence on God and to embrace absolute self-determination.

The fall of the cherub originated in his desire to be divine. Now he tempted the woman to experience the same, and he was successful. The center of human existence began to shift away from God toward itself. Eve was already experiencing something exciting: "The woman saw that the fruit of the tree was good for food and pleasing to the eye, and also desirable for gaining wisdom" (verse 6). This text contains several important ideas that we need to explore. First, the woman concluded that the fruit of the tree "was good." The biblical author uses the phrase "saw that it was good" throughout Genesis 1 to summarize God's opinion concerning His creation (Gen. 1:10, 12, 18, 21, and 25). Apparently Eve now assumed the divine role in evaluating a fragment of creation and concluding that it was good. But we find an important difference here. In the case of God, He simply declared the goodness of His creation. With Eve, however, it was good as a means to achieve something for her. One could say that the "good has become debased in the woman's mind. Its definition is no longer God's verdict but is rooted in the appeal to the senses and in utilitarian value. Egotism, greed, and self-interest now govern human nature."[2]

Second, Eve was not only corrupting the goodness of creation—she was also redefining creation's role. God had told her that the tree was not good for food, that its purpose in the garden was not to nurture them but to highlight the fact that they were free. She now examined the tree and assigned to it a new role, and in doing that she relegated to herself a divine prerogative. Over against the boundaries and the separation of functions that God assigned to the different elements of His creation, and particularly to the tree of good and evil, Eve declared that the tree was good *as food*—that eating of it would enrich her life.

Third, Eve concluded that the tree "was desirable [*chāmad*] for gaining wisdom [*śākal*]." She had now initiated a search for wisdom independent of God and propelled by greediness. Perhaps more important, the source of wisdom was

39

no longer God but creation itself, something accessible to humans apart from the "fear of the Lord" (cf. Prov. 1:7). Genesis 2:9 had used the verb *chāmad* to refer to the trees of the garden that were good for food as being of "desirable/delightful appearance." Now the biblical writer employs the same verb to describe the desirability of the tree of knowledge of good and evil as a means of wisdom. It is true that the natural world is one of God's means of revelation, but in this case Eve perverted it in the sense that she sundered creation from God and sought to turn it into a means to satisfy her selfish desires. Adam and Eve accepted self-existence apart from God. They misused their freedom by choosing an illusion.

Results of the Fall

The couple's act of rebellion against God expressed itself through eating of the tree. They had indeed chosen, but their choice was vacuous. From God's view there were only two options and nothing else. Therefore, the humans had in fact chosen death, not life, because to align themselves with the fallen cherub was a rejection of life.

Social disruption. By claiming independence from God, the human couple destroyed the center that made it possible for them to coexist harmoniously with themselves. There was not an inner center of gravity or balance to preserve the order established by God at the Creation. Each human became her or his own gravitational center in a desperate search for self-preservation or self-existence. In an unanticipated turn of events, Adam and Eve found the presence of each other threatening. Harmonious coexistence perished. In an eye-opening experience they realized that they were naked (Gen. 3:7). According to Genesis 2:25, nakedness without shame was the natural condition of humans in the Garden of Eden. The goodness of creation did not require them to mediate their presence to each other through garments.[3] They, as an expression of God's creation, did not need any material additions to improve their appearance, to be acceptable to the other. But sin permanently ruined that original condition, and they became aware of their nakedness. Their relationship was not as before—they now felt shame. Shame occurs in the presence of the other and reveals a disruption of social harmony.

Disruption of nature. The selfishness that after the Fall characterized humans now led them to exploit nature. Adam and Eve searched within the natural world for a way to handle their shame and guilt. They "sewed fig leaves together and made coverings for themselves" (Gen. 3:7). As a result, they began to divest nature of its natural beauty by using it in a way that God had not intended. In the process they damaged the natural world. This damage was more significant than they would have ever imagined. Paul describes the impact of sin and evil on nature as a type of slavery: "For the creation was subjected to frustration, not by its own choice, but by the will of the one who subjected it" to "bondage of decay" (Rom. 8:20, 21). The Greek term translated "frustration" (*mataiotēs*) means "vanity," "nothingness." Paul personifies nature and describes it as existing in a meaningless condition, under the power of someone else, and dying. Something strange happened to nature: "The spirit of rebellion, to which he [Adam] himself had given entrance, extended throughout the animal creation. Thus not only the life of man, but the nature of the beasts, the trees of the forest, the grass of the field, the very air he breathed, all told the sad lesson of the knowledge of evil."[4]

Disruption of union with God. The entrance of sin into the human heart severed its union with God. Humans now perceived Him as their enemy, the ultimate threat to their existence. The serpent planted in the human mind the idea that the Creator hindered human development by limiting humans to a creaturely mode of life. After the Fall Adam and Eve were persuaded that God was indeed their enemy. When He searched for them, they tried to find refuge and protection from His threatening presence among the trees of the garden. But the divine call summoned them to appear before Him, and they had no choice but to answer Him: "I heard you . . . , and I was afraid because I was naked" (Gen. 3:10). Their guilty conscience distorted their understanding of God, and they now viewed Him as someone they must fear—the enemy from whom they had to escape. The reference to nakedness as their reason for hiding from the Lord meant that they were fully aware of their unworthiness before the Lord. No longer in the condition in which the Lord created them, they realized that the covering they had prepared for themselves was not good enough. It created a deep sense of guilt and fear. Since then humans have understood God to be their enemy, not their friend.

The history of religion reveals the astonishing fact that the multiplicity of religious acts performed by humans has fundamentally been an attempt to move the gods to love and accept them. Humans sacrificed to the gods their own children in a desperate attempt to pacify the deities. They ascribed to their gods human needs and then satisfied them through their offerings in order to demonstrate that they were worthy of the gods' love. Such a distorted view of God originated in the warped mind of the fallen cherub and spread to the warped consciousness of fallen human beings.

Loss of freedom. Adam and Eve rejected the Lordship of the Creator in a vain search for autonomy and became slaves of a corrupting power that worked in opposition to God. The couple carried on themselves the shame of defeat. In the Old Testament the ideas of nakedness and shame have particular significance in the context of defeat. Nakedness symbolizes captivity. It was a com-

41

mon practice in the ancient world to force the defeated army—the prisoners of war—to march naked and in shame to the city of the victorious king (e.g., Isa. 20:4; cf. Job 12:17, 19; 2 Chron. 28:15; Deut. 28:48).[5] I would suggest that the emphasis on the nakedness of Adam and Eve may also indicate that they had been defeated by the enemy and had become prisoners of war.

Slaves of Sin Through Death: Peter wrote: "For a man is a slave to whatever has mastered him" (2 Peter 2:19). Paul added: "Don't you know that when you offer yourselves to someone to obey him as slaves, you are slaves to the one whom you obey . . .?" (Rom. 6:16). Consequently, humans live "in slavery to impurity and to ever-increasing wickedness" (verse 19). After the Fall sin spread across the earth with alarming speed (Gen. 6:5, 11), indicating that it was impossible for any human being to escape from its power. Paul's dictum is indeed correct: "There is no one righteous, not even one; there is no one who understands, no one who seeks God" (Rom. 3:10, 11; cf. Ps. 14:3).

The Bible describes the human condition in a depressing way. The prophet Jeremiah refers to the human heart as "deceitful above all things and beyond cure. Who can understand it?" (Jer. 17:9). Sin controls humans to the point that their minds are hostile to God and they are unable to submit to His law (Rom. 8:7, 8). The image of God, although not totally obliterated in humans, has been seriously damaged (cf. Rom. 3:23). Human beings recognize that there is something strangely wrong with them, but they are unable to remedy it (cf. Jer. 13:23). They desperately want to have inner peace, to love and be loved, to be free from fear and emotional and physical pain, to be able to achieve their most noble aims for life without any hindrance. Yet even their best efforts lead only to a mixture of partial success and deep frustration. In their natural condition they are never fully satisfied with what they have achieved or with who they are. Sin has disoriented humans and left them in darkness and spiritually incapacitated. The grip of sin is so strong that by themselves they cannot break away from it. The human search for self-realization ended in a state or condition in which sin ruled over them as a royal despot depriving them of real life.

The deep connection between sin and death makes the human condition even more desperate. Paul commented: "sin entered the world through one man, and death through sin, and in this way death came to all men, because all sinned" (Rom. 5:12). When Adam and Eve sinned, the first casualty was not simply their natural life, but particularly their spiritual life—their union with God. Sin possessed their very existence, producing an existential condition characterized by disconnectedness—by death. All humanity is entangled in the universality of sin.

Romans 5:12 describes a universal phenomenon that touches all humanity as a result of the sin of one—Adam. We find no reference here to the imputation of Adam's sin to "all." While there is clearly an element of solidarity with him, it is one *in result,* not in the act. What he did, as representative of the human race, impacted his descendants. Paul does not speculate concerning the connection between the specific sin of Adam and the sin of all. He simply states that the act of one brought sin as a power into the world. Sin then brought death, and since human beings are born in a state of death—separated from God and in need of salvation—they are unable to overcome sin (cf. Rom. 8:6-8). For Paul death is the wages of sin (Rom. 6:23), and at the same time what makes sin inevitable—that is to say, what allows sin to reign over humans (Rom. 5:21, 17). Theologically, death "designates the spiritual-physical condition of humanity 'in Adam,' which came initially through the sin of Adam (Rom. 5:12-21; 1 Cor. 15:21, 22)."[6] Humans are by nature dead in their transgressions and sins (Eph. 2:1).

The fact that death has reached every human being makes all humanity sinners.[7] We should take Paul's statement at face value and conclude that "death came to all," with the result that "all sinned." Death, both spiritual and physical, as well as sin, are a universal phenomena. Since the sin of Adam brought both physical death and spiritual death as separation from God, sinning became inevitable or unavoidable for all of his descendents ("all sinned"; cf. Rom. 3:9, 10). It is only through Christ's work of atonement that humans can escape the power of sin and death.

Slaves of Evil Powers: The Fall has enslaved humans to evil powers. The Bible describes Satan as the prince of our world (John 12:31; 14:30; 16:11). Paul refers to the Gentiles as those who "were slaves to those who by nature are not gods" (Gal. 4:8), that is to say, to spiritual powers who pretend to be gods. John goes even further when he declares: "We know . . . that the whole world is under the control of the evil one" (1 John 5:19). The word "world" carries here a negative connotation, designating humanity in opposition to God. This human mass "stands in a state of alienation and condemnation characterized by darkness (John 1:5; 12:46), death (5:19-27; 8:37, 44), sin (8:21, 34), slavery (8:34-36), and falsehood (8:44)."[8] It is that world that is under the control of the evil one, unable to overcome him or to free itself from his power.

Fortunately, the Lord did not allow humans to come under the absolute control of evil forces. As a result of His plan to restore the human race to loving union with Him, He set limits to their power over human beings. As soon as Adam and Eve sinned, the Lord said to the woman and to the evil one, "I will put enmity between you and the woman" (Gen. 3:15). The two will coexist in a state of hostility, unable to work harmoniously with each other. It was part of the rules of engagement in the cosmic conflict on earth, giving humans the opportunity, if they so wished, to chose life with God and not death. So humanity exists in a state of tension, unable to always do what is good and at the same time hating the evil they practice.

43

Slaves of the Law: The distorted view of God led humans to become slaves of the law. Legalism is the result of the deep-rooted conviction that God is indeed an enemy that needs to be pacified and that we can do so by making ourselves worthy of His love. Sin has also affected the divine purpose for the law. In fact, the enemy of the Lord has constantly opposed the law of God, even misusing it to stimulate the fallen human nature to rebellion through disobedience to the commandment (Rom. 7:8). Through his opposition to God's holy law he manifested his resistance to the divinely established order and thus rejected God's system of government. Sinful human beings regard the law as a threat. Paul says that the law, through the work of the Spirit in the human heart, makes us aware of the fact that we are sinners (Rom. 3:20; 7:7), but it is totally incapable of giving us life (Gal. 3:21). Such a use of the law aggravates the human predicament in that while, on the one hand, humans have sought acceptance before the Lord through submission to the law, on the other hand that law condemns them before Him (cf. Rom. 4:15). As a result, they find themselves in a situation that makes it impossible to find a way out of their predicament through their own efforts, and yet they are constantly trying to do it by themselves. It is a nonsensical, self-imposed, and self-destructive slavery. But Scripture declares: "No one will be declared righteous in his [God's] sight by observing the law; rather, through the law we become conscious of sin" (Rom. 3:20). Only the redemptive work of Christ restores the law to its rightful place in the Christian experience and frees us from its condemnation (Rom. 3:31; 8:1-4; Gal. 3:13).

Conclusion

The origin of sin in the world remains in the Scripture without excuse and absolutely unnecessary. The Fall of Adam and Eve, created in the image of God, cannot be fully understood. We can only point, as in the case of Lucifer, to their misuse of their freedom and, therefore, to the strange phenomenon of creaturely self-corruption. The damage they caused was permanent and irreparable. They chose death. Their fall brought enslavement to a power beyond their control, heading the human race toward total extinction. Had not Christ intervened, the separation between God and humans would have been final.

---

[1] Ellen G. White also supports that one of the key issues in the narrative was human freedom. She wrote: "God had power to hold Adam back from touching the forbidden fruit; but had he done this, Satan would have been sustained in his charge against God's arbitrary rule. Man would not have been a free moral agent, but a mere machine" (*The Seventh-day Adventist Bible Commentary*, ed. Francis D. Nichol [Washington, D.C.: Review and Herald, 1976], Ellen G. White Comments, vol. 1, p. 1084).

[2] Nahum M. Sarna, *Jewish Publication Society Torah Commentary: Genesis* (Philadelphia: Jewish Publication Society, 1989), p. 25.

[3] An ancient Jewish and Christian tradition has Adam and Eve covered by a mantle of light; see Edgar Haulotte, *Symbolique du vêtement selong la Bible* (Aubier: Éditions Montaigne, 1966), pp. 186, 187. Ellen G. White supports it when she refers to "the garment of innocence, a covering from God, which surrounded them," or "the light of the garments of heavenly innocence," or "the clear and perfect light that . . . surrounded them" (*The Seventh-day Adventist Bible Commentary*, Ellen G. White Comments, vol. 1, p. 1084).

[4] Ellen G. White, *Education* (Mountain View, Calif.: Pacific Press, 1903), pp. 26, 27.

[5] H. Niehr, "*ʿĀrôm*," in *Theological Dictionary of the Old Testament*, vol. 11, p. 353.

[6] J. J. Scott, Jr., "Life and Death," in *Dictionary of Paul and His Letters*, p. 554.

[7] Thomas R. Schreiner, *Romans* (Grand Rapids: Baker, 1998), pp. 274-277; Otfried Hofius writes: "What the statement is saying is that as a result of the fact that sin came into the world through Adam, and death through sin, death now applies to all of us, for we all stand inescapably under the sign of this fact, and therefore we all have sinned" ("The Adam-Christ Antithesis and the Law," in *Paul and the Mosaic Law*, ed. James D. G. Dunn [Grand Rapids: Eerdmans, 1996], p. 184).

[8] D. Moody Smith, *New Testament Theology: The Theology of John* (Cambridge, Eng.: Cambridge University Press, 1995), p. 81.

4

ATONEMENT AND THE
Divine Initiative

Anticipating future events or possibilities is vital in the preservation of order and safety in society. Take, for instance, the flu pandemics. Three of them struck during the past century, the most devastating occurring in 1918. That one killed more than a half million Americans and an estimated 40 million people around the world. It usually takes the specialists six to eight months to brew a flu vaccine. That is too long when trying to defeat a potentially mortal enemy. Therefore different countries have developed plans in advance to be ready to deal with such situation if it arises. In fact, they know that it will happen, so it is simply a matter of time and of being ready for it. In the case of the origin of sin, God did not get taken by surprise.

God's Reaction: Dealing With the Problem

Couldn't God have avoided the problem of sin by not creating Lucifer? The question is a valid one. Since God is omniscient, He foreknew that some of His intelligent creatures would rebel against Him. Since He is omnipotent, we must conclude that sin and evil exist because He permitted them to do so. We have already argued that no causal connection exists between God and sin. I must acknowledge that it is practically impossible to provide a satisfactory answer to the question under discussion. Since the Bible does not explicitly address this issue, any attempt to answer that question must remain incomplete and would include an element of speculation as we try to fill in the gaps of knowledge. One could theorize that God could have done what the question suggests. However, I would assume that in order for God to be always who He is, He had to allow Lucifer to become what he wanted to be, namely, Satan.

When we try to guess what God would or would not have done, we have no choice but to use analogical language. That is to say, we have to use human language, experiences, and conditions—in other words, what we know—to attempt to

46

imagine what God could have done. With that in mind, let me make a suggestion for your consideration. It would be correct to state that at some moment in eternity God decided, in His own freedom, to create intelligent, free creatures. He also knew that one of those creatures would rebel against Him. Should not God at that moment second-guess His original decision and perhaps change His mind? From the human perspective the most rational response would be yes! By doing that, He would have aborted the origin of evil. Analogically we would expect God to arrive at the same conclusion and to change His plan. But we need to examine a little more carefully our prompt reaction.

We should ask ourselves, Why would we change our mind? The fundamental answer would probably be that we want to avoid a serious problem. The truth is that we would give up our plans because we fear facing a difficult problem. Hence, the problem we anticipated defeated us in the sense that it forced us to change what we had determined to do. But God is not like us! Once He decided to create intelligent, free creatures, there was no real or potential force able to force Him to alter His plans. When the Godhead saw the problem, the question that may have come to mind was not Should We change our plans? but How should We solve this problem? Otherwise, the fear of having to deal with rebellious creatures would have defeated Him in the sense of His feeling compelled to alter His plan. There is no power outside God's own nature capable of forcing Him to modify or abandon what He intends to do. A defeated God is not a true God. Our God is the Fearless One who, without changing His plan, decided to confront the problem of sin and evil so as to resolve it once and for all through His Son. Besides, imposing moral and spiritual sanctions on intelligent beings would have deprived them of their true freedom.

God's Reaction to Sin: Divine Grace

When the condition of the human race became desperate, God decided to restore it to divine favor through the redemptive work of His Son. In a sense we could say that God reacted to human sin in an unexpected way. Instead of withdrawing life—allowing His wrath to express itself— He released the creative energy of His grace. This grace, hidden within the depths of the divine essence, was at a particular moment discharged in order to re-create a world ruined by sin and rebellion. It is there that we find the origin of the atonement.

Grace and the Godhead. God's self-revelation to Moses firmly established that He is by nature gracious: "The Lord, the Lord, the compassionate and gracious God, slow to anger, abounding in love and faithfulness, maintaining love to thousands, and forgiving wickedness, rebellion and sin" (Ex. 34:6). The New Testament reaffirms the divine nature when it speaks about "the grace of our God and the Lord Jesus Christ" (2 Thess. 1:12). Grace—the desire to bestow unmerited favor or gifts—belongs to the very essence of the Father and the Son, in whom we find the fullness of grace (John 1:16). But Scripture also associates grace with the Spirit, whom it refers to as "the Spirit of grace" (Heb. 10:29), echoing the Old Testament (Zech. 12:10). We find the Spirit directly mentioned in the epistolary salutations, e.g., "Grace and peace to you from him who is, and who was, and who is to come, and from the seven spirits before his throne, and from Jesus Christ" (Rev. 1:4, 5). This last passage clearly connects grace with the three persons of the Godhead. Such an emphasis does not allow us to link grace exclusively to Christ, as if He had to persuade the other members of the Godhead to show grace to sinful human beings. Grace is a defining and determining dimension of the very being of God as a plurality of persons, and therefore there never existed a time that it was not a characteristic of any one of them. The overflow of grace toward human beings is a simultaneous experience and activity of the Father, the Son, and the Holy Spirit. This is theologically foundational for a biblical understanding of the atonement.

Grace as unmerited favor. In the Bible "grace" is God's benevolence and kindness toward sinners, a concept rooted in the use of the Hebrew words *chen* and *chesed* in the Old Testament. *Chesed* designates God's everlasting covenant love and His faithfulness, goodness, and graciousness (cf. Isa. 54:10; Jer. 31:3). His graciousness brings forgiveness to sinners (Micah 7:8) and delivers those in need of salvation (Ps. 6:4, 5). It often points to the kind of "spontaneous generosity with which He responds to the people of His covenant (e.g., 1 Kings 8:23; Isa. 55:3; Ps. 89:29, 50; 106:45)" and which is "a harbinger of the grace that appeared bringing salvation to all people in Christ (Titus 2:11)."[1] In fact, God's unfailing love fills the whole earth (Ps. 33:5).[2]

The Hebrew term *chen* designates "grace" and "favor" and in general it refers "to the positive disposition one person has toward another."[3] More specifically, grace found expression in acts of benevolence "shown by the rich toward the poor, or at least by an individual with means toward one who has little or no means."[4] Divine grace goes even beyond the human expression of grace. God's grace is available to the righteous (Gen. 6:8, 9) and the repentant (Isa. 30:19), but He also shows it to the unrepentant (Neh. 9:17, 31). In the Old Testament "God's grace is finally rooted, not in what people do, but in his disposition to be gracious in ways beyond any human formula or calculations (Ex. 33:19; 34:6)."[5]

The word *charis*, often translated as "grace" in the New Testament, in the Greek world designated "a beneficent disposition toward someone, *favor, grace, gracious care/help, goodwill.*"[6] People commonly employed it in the sense of favor and goodwill.[7] When used to refer to "a quality of benevolence that gives favor to inferiors,"[8] *charis* came very close to expressing its New Testament content. Anytime that God or Christ is the subject of grace, that is to say, whenever they are "acting in grace toward human kind, it is undeserved favor."[9] Grace is divine generosity, unmerited favor from God to sinners. It is not motivated by human goodness, and humans do not have a claim on it. Rather, it flows from the loving heart of God to those who are unworthy. He shows His glorious grace to those who are dead in their transgressions (Eph. 2:5) and who have fallen "short of the glory of God" (Rom. 3:23). Furthermore, grace takes the initiative and goes out searching for sinners, offering them what they do not deserve, namely, divine kindness and acceptance. A particular expression of God's loving nature, it is divine love toward rebellious creatures that do not deserve it.[10] While sin does not activate divine grace, covenant breaking "provides the occasion for its demonstration."[11]

Grace and Christ. Divine grace is not something abstract and difficult to comprehend with our intellect. In the New Testament such grace is a visible reality because it is embodied in Christ in its fullness (John 1:16). Through the incarnation and ministry of Christ we confront the epiphany of God's grace: "For the grace of God has appeared, bringing salvation to all men" (Titus 2:11, NASB). The kindness and the free gift of salvation from God reached us in His own person. In a sense we could say that He did not bring grace, but that He was the grace of God in human form. For Paul the grace of God is Jesus Christ (Rom. 5:15). He adds: "For you know the grace of our Lord Jesus Christ, that though he was rich, yet for your sakes he became poor, so that you through his poverty might become rich" (2 Cor. 8:9). The grace of Christ consisted in becoming what we are in order for us to participate in what He had. His self-sacrificing nature of grace became particularly visible at the moment that grace hung on the cross of Calvary (Gal. 2:21).

Since the Christ event was the unique expression of grace, the New Testament equates grace with the gospel of salvation (Acts 20:24), also called "the word of his grace" (verse 32). In the proclamation of that message grace "is reaching more and more people" (2 Cor. 4:15). The inevitable conclusion is that grace is available to all exclusively in and through Christ. It is only through Him that "we have gained access by faith into this grace in which we now stand" (Rom. 5:2). We read that God's grace was "given you in Christ Jesus" (1 Cor. 1:4), or that it has been "freely given us in the One he [God] loves" (Eph. 1:6). Second Timothy 1:9, 10 beautifully expresses the fundamental theological significance of the connection between grace and Christ: "This grace was given us in Christ Jesus before the beginning of time, but it has now been revealed through the appearing of our Savior, Christ Jesus, who has destroyed death and has brought life and immortality to light through the gospel." The divine initiative to save us took place "before the beginning of time," when the Godhead determined that grace was going to be provided for us exclusively in Christ. God has overcome death through the power of grace as His unmerited favor to undeserving, sinful human beings.

49

Divine Provision: An Eternal Plan

God not only anticipated the emergence of sin but also prepared a way out of it. The Bible refers to His divine act as a "mystery," not in the modern sense of something beyond comprehension, but as something beyond human creativity, understanding, and accessibility, but that has been now revealed. We should explore more carefully the nature of that mystery.

God preordained it. The divine mind conceived the mystery. No creature had the wisdom to configure a plan that would effectively address the problem of sin and evil. First Corinthians 2:7 associates this mystery with divine wisdom and describes it as something preordained (Greek *proorizō*, "to predestine," "to decide beforehand") by God. He not only defined the nature of the mystery, but also established that it would take place. No one would be able to thwart the divine intention for us. Therefore the divine mystery is an expression of "his will, according to his good pleasure, which he purposed . . ." (Eph. 1:9). What God determined to do was not something imposed on Him from the outside, but what He voluntarily willed, thus shaping the future by His will "according to his good pleasure." The Greek term translated "good pleasure," *eudokia*, refers to the goodwill of a person, to his or her kind disposition. God's decision was an expression of His goodness. The divine mystery also had purpose to it. Not an irrational decision, it came from the divine wisdom with specific intention.

A hidden mystery. The divine mystery was a well-kept secret within the Godhead. The New Testament states that this mystery was "kept hidden in God, who created all things" (Eph. 3:9; cf. 1 Cor. 2:7), or that the mystery "has been kept hidden for ages and generations" (Col. 1:26). Those passages indicate not only that this mystery originated in God, but that there existed a time that it was totally unnecessary for His creatures to know about it. In fact, the reason for using the word "mystery" is that in the Bible a mystery is something kept secret or hidden for a period of time. It presupposes an understanding of history based on a divine plan for His creatures. God has established things that, although for a time are not clearly disclosed, at a particular moment will be revealed.

Christ as the mystery of God. What is the content of this mystery? According to Colossians 2:2, 3, it is Christ: "the mystery of God, namely, Christ, in whom are hidden all the treasures of wisdom and knowledge." Long before God created anything, the Godhead configured this glorious mystery that consisted in the coming of God in human flesh into the history of sin and death on our planet. First Timothy 3:16 clearly describes this reality: "Beyond all question, the mystery of godliness is great: He appeared in a body, was vindicated by the Spirit, was seen by angels, was preached among the nations, was believed on in the world, was taken up in glory." In other words, the mystery that provides the basis for a godly life is the person and work of Christ for the human race—His incarnation, ministry, and exaltation. The mystery is not an abstract idea that we are simply called to grasp intellectually, but the very person of God as He appeared within human history and the redemptive power of that divine epiphany.

It is that redemptive dimension of Christ as the mystery of God emphasized in Ephesians 1:9, 10, particularly when the apostle declares that the mystery was set forth in Christ "to bring all things in heaven and on earth together under one head, even Christ." The divine mystery, Christ, has a cosmic function. Sin fragmented the universe, now God is reuniting, and the place that the reunification of the cosmos is taking place is in the person of Christ. The reconciling effectiveness of Christ as God's mystery, hidden for ages in God, is so encompassing that Paul equates the mystery with the gospel itself (Rom. 16:25, 26). But in order to establish that the mystery is a person, the apostle will describe the appropriation of the mystery as the indwelling of Christ in the life of the believer (Col. 1:27).

Specific elements of the mystery. The New Testament mentions some specific aspects of the divine mystery, all of them related to the nature and work of Christ, the supreme manifestation of that mystery. As we already mentioned, it includes our incorporation into Christ in order to participate in "the glorious riches of this mystery" (Col. 1:27). It also involves, among other things, the Christian teachings (1 Tim. 3:9), the eschatological consummation of the work of Christ that is yet fully to be revealed (Rev. 10:7), the full transformation of Christians at the moment of the return of Christ (1 Cor. 15:51), God's eschatological plan for Israel (Rom. 11:25), and the glorification of believers (1 Cor. 2:7). God fixed all of those elements in eternity as part of His secret plan in Christ, and consequently they will take effect as He purposed.

Revelation and proclamation of the mystery. Humans come to know the divine mystery through divine revelation. Human wisdom is not good enough to uncover or unveil what God hid in Himself. But the prophets announced the mystery—that is to say, they proclaimed on behalf of God that He would fulfill His plan within history (cf. Rev. 10:7; Rom. 16:26). The experience of Daniel well illustrates the prophets' involvement in the revelation of the mystery of God. The book of Daniel calls the dream of the king, something that human wisdom could not reconstruct and explain, a "mystery" (Dan. 2:18). The original Aramaic word is *rāz* ("secret"), translated into Greek as *mystērion* ("mystery"). The dream was a revelation of a divine mystery totally beyond human control or access. Daniel and his companions prayed and "during the night the mystery was revealed to Daniel in a vision" (verse 19). They learned what God had decreed would happen in the course of human history (verse 28), specifically the future (verse 45). The "*mystērion* in Daniel contains what remains of human history and is particularly focused on God's eschatological act of subjecting all under His dominion. Moreover, even that part of human history that will yet unfold, with all that it may entail for God's people, is part of God's purpose."[12] The dream was a partial disclosure of the divine mystery that in the future God would fully unveil (Dan. 12:9).

Then, at the proper time God made the mystery public in Christ, who "was chosen before the creation of the world, but was revealed in these last times for your sake" (1 Peter 1:20; cf. Gal. 4:4). The event of Christ is "now revealed and made known through the prophetic writings by the command of the eternal God" (Rom. 16:26). In other words, Christ as the revelation of the mystery of God is in conformity with the prophetic revelation. God has "made known to us the mystery of his will . . . , which he purposed in Christ" (Eph. 1:9). It was "revealed by the Spirit to God's holy apostles and prophets" (Eph. 3:5). Paul specifically says that God "made known" the mystery to him "by revelation" (verse 3) and that it "is now disclosed to the saints" (Col. 1:26). The divine mystery reaches us as a disclosure from God and not as the result of human activity. It is the responsibility of believers to proclaim it to all. They are now bearers of the divine mystery (1 Cor. 2:7; Eph. 2:19; Col. 1:27; 4:3), stewards of the mysteries of God (1 Cor. 4:1).

Summarizing, at some point in eternity the Godhead determined to deal with the sin problem through Jesus Christ. This is the mystery that God hid within Himself through the ages until the time came for Him to disclose it in the context of a world of sin and rebellion. By placing the decision of the plan of salvation before Creation Scripture indicates that God voluntarily and out of His own nature and love determined that He was going to restore humanity to harmony with Him. The life and ministry of Christ revealed that God was fulfilling the divine plan as He intended in the arena of human history.

Christ's Submission to the Divine Plan

The coming of Christ to our world was indispensable in implementing the divine plan. From beginning to end He fulfilled the divine intention for His life in human flesh. In his sermon on Pentecost Peter indicated that in the ministry of Jesus God was totally active, that Jesus was handed over to the Jewish leaders "by God's set purpose and foreknowledge; and you, with the help of wicked men, put him to death by nailing him to the cross. But God raised him from the dead, freeing him from the agony of death, because it was impossible for death to keep its hold on him" (Acts 2:23, 24). The apostle added that God exalted Him to His right hand and that "God has made this Jesus . . . both Lord and Christ" (verse 36). God was active and present in a unique way in Jesus Christ.

Acting out God's plan. What Christ achieved for the human race was possible because He came and fulfilled His mission in obedience to the eternal plan. We see this particularly emphasized by the impersonal Greek verb *dein* ("it is necessary," "one must," "one has to"), employed quite often in conjunction with the redemptive activities of Jesus. In Greek literature the religious use of this verb often refers to the force of fate that is inescapable and imposes itself on the world. The biblical writers, who thought of "God in terms of the will which personally summons man and which fashions history according to its plan,"[13] rejected such an impersonal or neutral necessity or fate. In Scripture the ground for the necessity is theologically speaking the divine will.[14] Such is the case in the Old Testament, which regards submission to the law as an expression of God's will, as a duty (e.g., Lev. 5:17, LXX), and in the New Testament, in which the "will of God known to the Christian community lays duties upon it and upon the individual Christian" who is expected to live by it (e.g., 1 Thess. 4:1; 1 Tim. 3:2, 7, 15; Titus 1:7).[15]

But the verb *dei* carries with it the idea of a divine plan that needs to be carried out and that will become effectual in human history. We find the root of this understanding in biblical apocalyptic thought,[16] specifically in Daniel 2:28, 29, in which the prophet reports to the Babylonian ruler the dream and its meaning. He tells the king that God showed him "what will happen in days to come" (verse 28) or "what is going to happen" (verse 29). The Greek version of the Old Testament (LXX) used in those two passages the verb *dei*: "What is necessary to/must happen." The verb came to have an eschatological content designating the established ordering of eschatological events "up to and including the last days" and their inevitability.[17] In the New Testament this verb "is normally an expression for the decree and especially of the plan of God."[18]

That divine plan became effectual in and through Christ, whose necessity to fulfill it shaped His whole life. The New Testament applies the verb *dei* to a variety of situations in the life of Jesus. First, it qualifies the travels of Jesus. It is necessary for Him to go to the house of Zacchaeus (Luke 19:5), to pass by Samaria (John 4:4), to be in His Father's house (Luke 2:49), to be constantly traveling (Luke 12:33), and to go up to Jerusalem (Matt. 16:21). All of His moves were motivated by the need to do God's will as He followed the divine plan for the human race. Second, Jesus stated that it was necessary for Him to preach the good news to the cities "because that is why I was sent" (Luke 4:43). He needed to "do the work of him who sent me" (John 9:4) and to bring in the sheep that are not of His pen in order to have one fold and one shepherd (John 10:16). The drive to proclaim the good news of the kingdom of God determined the divine compulsion to visit places and people. It also moved Paul to proclaim the gospel in Rome (Acts 23:11).

Third, he announced some events required to take place before the end. The gospel would need to be preached to every nation (Mark 13:10). Wars and rumors of wars are things that "must happen, but the end is still to come" (verse 7; cf. Matt. 24:6; Luke 21:9). Other New Testament writers will use the verb *dei* to refer to eschatological events that must occur according to the divine plan. John refers to the eschatological events discussed in Revelation as that which "must soon [it is necessary to] take place" (Rev. 1:1; cf. 4:1; 22:6). More specifically, he mentions the need to prophesy again (Rev. 10:11), for the kings to remain for a little while (Rev. 17:10), and for Satan to be loosed for a little while (Rev. 20:3). Paul refers to the end-time judgment, saying, "For we must all appear before the judgment seat of Christ" (2 Cor. 5:10). At the second coming of Christ, "the perishable must clothe itself with the imperishable, and the mortal with immortality" (1 Cor. 15:53). All of those events are directly connected with or are the result of the submission of Christ to the divine plan unavoidably being fulfilled in human history.

Fourth, the passion of Jesus stood at the heart of the divine plan and was something that He had to do in order to redeem the human race. It was unavoidable for Him to go up to Jerusalem, to be rejected, to suffer, and to be killed (Matt. 16:21; Mark 8:31; Luke 9:22). He said to the disciples, "The Son of Man must [needs to] be delivered into the hands of sinful men" (Luke 24:7), and that "just as Moses lifted up the snake in the desert, so the Son of Man must [needs to] be lifted up, that everyone who believes in him may have eternal life" (John 3:14, 15; cf. 12:34). Because of the suffering of Christ, even the suffering of believers has been incorporated into the divine plan (e.g., Acts 4:12; 16:30). The passion of the Lord was part of the eternal mystery hidden within the Godhead and now made visible on the cross. But it in no way exempted the human perpetrators from culpability. Their action and the divine plan coincided, but they remained guilty of their crime.

Fifth, if Christ's death was something He had to experience, so was also His resurrection. His announcements of the passion included the resurrection from the dead as something that "must [it was necessary to] happen" (e.g., Mark 8:31; Luke 24:7). Paul proclaimed that "Christ had [it was necessary] to suffer and rise from the dead" (Acts 17:3). John adds a new element when he says, concerning the disciples, that "they still did not understand from Scripture that Jesus had [was necessary] to rise from the dead" (John 20:9). The necessity is now grounded in the prophetic nature and authority of the Scriptures. The reason is that they announced the actualization of the divine plan in the life of the Messiah. God had in Scripture established and determined that Jesus would be resurrected from the dead and that it would happen as predicted in the life of the Savior. The result was that His tomb is now absolutely empty!

Sixth, it was necessary for Him not only to suffer but also to "enter his glory" (Luke 24:26). Here the text refers both to His resurrection and to His ascension. Heaven is His new locality, and "he must remain" there "until the time comes for God to restore everything, as he promised long ago through his holy prophets" (Acts 3:21). At the Ascension He took His place at the right hand of the Father, and "he must [it is necessary for him to] reign until he has put all his enemies under his feet" (1 Cor. 15:25). The enthronement of Christ and His final victory over the forces of evil were not left to chance, but were predetermined in the divine council as events that needed to occur within the flow of redemptive history.

Thus the use of the verb *dei* in conjunction with the life and experiences of Jesus indicates that His very being remained under the compulsion of a self-sacrificing love that did not stop at anything in order to fulfill the divine plan for the salvation of a sinful race. The determinism that characterizes the apocalyptic prophecies of the Bible was in a sense incarnated in the life and work of Christ. Obviously it does not mean that Jesus was a puppet controlled by forces stronger than Him. His submission to the divine plan was a voluntary act on His part. That apocalyptic determinism is mysteriously operative within human history, leading it to the establishing of the kingdom of God. Apocalyptic thinking unquestionably oriented Christ's ministry.

Conclusion

The Bible calls God's loving disposition to sinners, who do not deserve kindness, divine grace. Out of that grace God designed a plan to rescue the human race from sin's enslaving and destructive power. God preordained it, but it remained hidden in the mystery of the Godhead until the moment that humans fell into sin. Then God began to reveal it to them in a variety of ways. At the appropriate moment the Godhead fully implemented it in and through the person of the Son of God. Throughout His ministry on earth Christ was implementing the divine plan for the salvation of sinners. It reached its culmination in His willing submission to His death on the cross.

---

[1] L. B. Smedes, "Grace," in *International Standard Bible Encyclopedia*, ed. Geoffrey W. Bromiley (Grand Rapids: Eerdmans, 1982), vol. 2, p. 549.

[2] It has been correctly stated that the use of *chesed* in the Old Testament expands from the realm of "the fellowship of family and clan to the nation of Israel and finally to the whole world" (H.-J. Zobel, "*Chesed*," in *Theological Dictionary of the Old Testament*, vol. 5, p. 63).

[3] D. N. Freedman and J. R. Lundbom, "*Chānan*," in *Theological Dictionary of the Old Testament*, vol. 5, p. 24.

[4] *Ibid.*, p. 28.

[5] Terence E. Fretheim, "*Chnn*," in *New International Dictionary of the Old Testament Theology and Exegesis*, vol. 2, p. 205.

[6] Danker, *Greek-English Lexicon*, p. 1079.

[7] Conzelmann, "*Charis*," *Theological Dictionary of the New Testament*, vol. 9, p. 374.

[8] Smedes, "Grace," in *International Standard Bible Encyclopedia*, vol. 2, p. 548. See also K. Berger, "*Charis*, grace, gratitude; esteem," in *Exegetical Dictionary of the New Testament*, vol. 3, p. 457, who comments that the term "is used in non-Christian writings to refer to both 'generosity' and 'gratitude,' and also to 'gracefulness' and 'beauty'—thus to free, uncoerced, cheerfully bestowed openness toward one another, and thus in relationship to God both 'salvation' granted by him and human 'thanks.' Aristotle [*Rhetoric* 2. 7. 1385a) already emphasizes the gratuitous nature of *charis* in contrast to reward."

[9] A. B. Luter, Jr., "Grace," in *Dictionary of Paul and His Letters*, p. 372.

[10] Indeed, "the whole concept of grace lies at the heart of Paul's soteriology and in that connection we note that 'the grace of God' 'denotes an essential feature of God's love. When applied to God, the word grace denotes the favor of God toward those who do not deserve his favor, . . .

God is seen as one who bestows unmerited favor on the objects of his love. . . . Grace is another name for the outgoing character of his love, especially to sinners and to his elect people" (D. Guthrie and R. P. Martin, "God," in *Dictionary of Paul and His Letters*, p. 364).

[11] M. S. Horton, *Lord and Servant*, p. 60. Ellen G. White comments, "We would never have learned the meaning of this word 'grace' had we not fallen. God loves the sinless angels who do His service and are obedient to all His commands, but He does not give them grace. These heavenly beings know naught of grace; they have never needed it, for they have never sinned. Grace is an attribute of God shown to undeserving human beings. We did not seek after it, but it was sent in search of us. God rejoices to bestow this grace on everyone who hungers for it, not because we are worthy, but because we are so utterly unworthy. Our need is the qualification which gives us the assurance that we will receive this gift" (*My Life Today* [Washington, D.C.: Review and Herald, 1952], p. 100).

[12] Chrys C. Caragounis, *The Ephesian Mysterion: Meaning and Content* (Sweden: CWK Gleerup, 1977), p. 124.

[13] Walter Grundmann, "*Dei*," in *Theological Dictionary of the New Testament*, vol. 2, p. 22.

[14] W. Popkes, "*Dei*, It Is Necessary," in *Exegetical Dictionary of the New Testament*, vol. 1, p. 279.

[15] Grundmann, p. 21.

[16] W. J. Bennett, Jr., "The Son of Man Must . . . ," *Novum Testamentum* 17 (1975): 119-124.

[17] *Ibid.*, pp. 120, 122.

[18] Popkes.

5

ATONEMENT
Announced

The mystery of God was announced as soon as sin came into the world. At that moment it was a promise of salvation whose full benefits sinners could appropriate only through faith in the coming Savior. Many passages in the Old Testament reveal aspects of the divine plan to the people of God. Here we can deal with only a limited number of them, selected on the basis of their overall importance in anticipating the nature and results of Christ's atoning work.

The Seed of the Woman

God foreshadowed the divine plan for the salvation of the human race to Adam and Eve immediately after the Fall, while they were still in the Garden of Eden. The Lord said: "I will put enmity between you and the woman, and between your offspring and hers; he will crush your head, and you will strike his heel" (Gen. 3:15). Christians have called it the *protevangelium* ("early gospel"), that is to say, the first announcement of the gospel of salvation to humanity. Several factors point to a messianic reading of the text.

The serpent and the enemy of God. First, in the context of the narrative the serpent stands for something more important than a simple reptile. It is fundamentally an anti-God power whose main role in the narrative is to misrepresent God and to invite others to rebel against Him. Scripture elsewhere identifies Satan as "the ancient serpent called the devil" (Rev. 12:9). As we previously indicated, what was good the enemy of the Creator now misused. It was part of the cosmic conflict whose origin predated the creation of the human race.

Enmity between the woman and the serpent. Second, the enmity, or antagonism, is something that the Creator places between the serpent and the woman. God wills that a constant conflict exist between the two of them. As indicated, that enmity implies that the relationship between humans and the serpent will never be harmonious. The evil power will not totally or absolutely enslave human beings, even though it overcame them. In other words, the enmity places limits to the control of the evil over humanity. In this way God preserves human freedom, indispensable in the fulfillment of the divine plan of salvation for the human race.

Collective and singular use of *zera*. Third, another factor that points to the messianic reading of the text is that the term *zera* ("seed, descendants") does not always express a collective meaning. In a number of cases it refers to a particular individual. For instance, in Genesis 4:25 Eve says, "God has granted me another child [*zera*, "seed"] in place of Abel." The word "seed" specifies Seth and is not a collective noun. The parallel in Genesis 15:3 between "seed" and "heir" also suggests that we are dealing with an individual. Later God identifies Ishmael as the offspring/seed of Abraham (Gen. 21:13; see also 38:8, 9). One of the best examples of the use of "seed" in the singular appears in 1 Samuel 1:11. As Hannah prays for a son she asks the Lord to "give her a son [literally, "seed of men"], then I will give him to the Lord" (cf. 1 Sam. 2:20). In this case the antecedent of the singular pronoun "him" is the "seed/son," indicating that the noun *zera* designates a specific descendant. The same applies to Solomon, called the "descendant" of David (2 Sam. 7:12). They are all immediate descendants of a particular person.

In the case of Genesis 3:15 the collective use is present, but at the same time the possibility of a reference to an individual descendant is not ruled out, as suggested by the common translation of the last part of the verse as "*he* will crush your head, and you will strike *his* feet." The question is whether we should interpret the singular pronoun as a collective and translate it "they" or "it." The fact that "seed" could designate an individual and that our passage employs a singular pronoun suggests that we are dealing with an ambiguity; therefore the reference could be to both a specific descendant and the descendants as a whole of the woman.

Final victory over the serpent. Fourth, a messianic reading of Genesis 3:15 indicates that the conflict between the seed of the woman and that of the serpent will come to an end. The passage contains both judgment and good news. The phrase "he will crush your head, and you will strike his heel" anticipates the ultimate defeat of evil. The verb translated "crush" is the same verb translated "strike" (Heb. *shûph*), and that raises the question of the proper translation. The main problem is that the verb appears in only two other passages (Ps. 139:11 and Job 9:17), and even there its meaning is not clear. One could suggest that "to strike at" would express the basic idea of the verb and that the intensity of the strike would depend on the object that receives it.[1] Since the serpent aims at the heel it only "bruises" or "snaps at" it, while an assault to the head intends "to crush" the serpent's head and could be mortal.

If the passage does not include a victory, then what we have is a perpetual battle between good and evil. In that case the curse would be not only against the serpent but also against humans. Consequently "the man and the woman are punished twice over" and the serpent receives "a lesser punishment than that imposed upon the human couple."[2] Such a reading is foreign to the text.

Significance of the word "seed." Fifth, one should not overlook the fact that the topic of the "seed/descendent(s)" will play a significant role in the rest of the book of Genesis. The singular and the collective uses almost merge into each other as history moves forward in the patriarchal narratives. The promises made to one also go to the others. It is not only about the preservation of the existence of God's people, but also about the fulfillment of His promises. Eve was concerned with the loss of her seed/son Abel, but the Lord gave her another seed/son, Seth (Gen. 4:25). The covenant that God made with Noah included also his future descendants (Gen. 9:9). The covenant promises are the force driving history through the descendants and become a more significant theological topic in the life of Abraham.

In order for God to fulfill His purposes for the human race, He chose Abram and his descendants (Gen. 12:7). To him and to his descendants God promised both the land (Gen. 13:15) and to make them innumerable, like the dust of the earth (verse 16). The promises were oriented toward the future. The need for a descendant, a son, came to play a mayor role in the stories. Abram suspected that because he did not have a son, Eliezer, his servant, would become his heir (Gen. 15:3). But the Lord assured him of a son (verse 4). Now the promise of descendants and the promise of a son merged into each other. This promise of a descendant as well as future descendants who will be as numerous as the stars (Gen. 15:5; 22:17) will now drive the course of history. The future was the place where the promises would see their fulfillment. It would include the time of slavery in Egypt, Israel's deliverance from there, and the giving of the land to them (Gen. 15:13, 18). The covenant that the Lord made with Abraham was a permanent one because it included his descendants (Gen. 17:7-10). The promises would meet their fulfillment through Isaac, Abraham's son/seed (Gen. 17:19; 21:12). His seed/descendants were to overcome their enemies and to become a blessing to the nations of the earth (Gen. 22:17; 12:18; 24:60). The fulfillment of the promises through the seed of Abraham would shape history (Gen. 24:7). That is the meaning of the constant renewal of the promises of descendants and of the land to Isaac (Gen. 26:3, 4, 24), and Jacob (Gen. 28:4; 32:12; 48:4). In a particular way, the promises began to mold history when the sons of Jacob increased and went to Egypt (Gen. 46:6, 7; cf. 48:11, 19). This future-oriented understanding of the seed/descendants of Abraham is grounded in the future-oriented nature of the seed of the woman in Genesis 3:15.

An interest in the descendant/descendants through whom God will fulfill His promises runs throughout the Old Testament and reaches into the New Testament. In the Old Testament the connection of the descendant/son with David and his dynasty becomes particularly important. Scripture employs the plural and the singular in an almost fluid way. The Lord will rise up a son/descendant of David and will establish his dynasty after him (2 Sam. 7:12, 16). The promise of a descendant of David who will always sit on the throne gets repeated in other passages (e.g., 1 Kings 2:33; 11:39). The Lord said to David, "I will establish your line [zera^c] forever and make your throne firm through all generations" (Ps. 89:4; see also verses 29 and 36). Through the Davidic dynasty the enemies of Israel would meet their defeat (2 Sam. 22:38-41; cf. Ps. 89:23, 24), the promise of the land would receive its fulfillment, and its enemies would "lick the dust" (see Ps. 72:8, 9).[3] In the New Testament He who will sit on the throne of David is Jesus, the son of God and the Son of David (Luke 1:31-33; Mark 10:47); the one "who as to his human nature was a descendant [literally, "from the seed"] of David" (Rom. 1:3).

Genesis 3:15 and the New Testament. Sixth, we find in the New Testament allusions to Genesis 3:15 in the context of the work of Jesus and His people. The New Testament describes the serpent as an evil, deceptive power (Rev. 12:9) in the context of a revelatory experience that represents the people of God as a woman, Jesus as her son, and the end-time children of the woman as the "remnant of her seed" (verses 5, 6, 17, KJV). Here the descendant of the woman is Jesus and at the same time the children of God. The seed of the woman, Jesus Christ (Rev. 20:10), who had also defeated him on the cross (Rev. 12:10), finally destroys the serpent or dragon.

Another allusion to Genesis 3:15 appears in Romans 16:20, in which Paul writes: "The God of peace will soon crush Satan under your feet." The reference is not exclusively to the defeat of false teachers, but extends "to the final eschatological victory of God's people when Satan is thrown into the 'lake of fire.'"[4] God's people participate in His victory over the evil one. Since this will happen through His Son, then the one and the many are inseparable in that the victory of the one is also the victory of His brothers and sisters (1 Cor. 15:25, 26).

When we place Genesis 3:15 within the witness of the totality of the Scripture, its messianic content becomes clear. The promise was the first indication of a plan for the redemption of sinners, one formulated within the mystery of the Godhead. From the perspective of the New Testament it becomes clear that Genesis 3:15 pointed to a time when the Son of the woman, who is the Son of God, will overcome once and for all the forces of evil and bring peace between God and humanity.

God Clothed Them

The goodness of God toward fallen human beings we see demonstrated in the merciful act of dressing them: "The Lord God made garments of skin for Adam and his wife and clothed them" (verse 21). The emphasis is on the divine activity. The passage, within its context, "contains a surprise. The cursed ones are protected. The one who *tests* is the one who finally *provides* (Gen. 3:2; cf. 22:1-14). With the sentence given, God does (3:21) for the couple what they cannot do for themselves (3:7). They cannot deal with their shame. But God can, will, and does. To be clothed is to be given life (cf. Gen. 37:3, 23, 32; 2 Cor. 5:4). But the creatures cannot clothe themselves, nor finally each other."[5] The passage contains an embryonic message of salvation.

But it can also tempt one to read too much into it, creating the danger of overlooking important aspects of its message. One of the details easily missed is that God made the garments out of the skin of animals. Contextually, the contrast is between what Adam and Eve did, i.e., dressed themselves with "fig leaves" (Gen. 3:7), and God Himself dressing them with "garments of skin."

The text implies that at least an animal died in order to provide what Eve and Adam needed, namely, the gift of a garment that would remove their shame and allow them to stand before the Lord. If it is true that the divine act of dressing them meant granting them life, then that life was possible because of the life of another, in this case an animal, given for theirs. The passage implies a sacrificial victim and that it took the place of the sinner. The New Testament bases the effectiveness of the sacrificial offerings of the Old Testament on the conviction that Christ is "the Lamb that was slain from the creation of the world" (Rev. 13:8). As soon as sin appeared on our planet, the divine plan entered into effect through types pointing to the coming sacrificial ministry of Jesus.

Abraham's Sacrifice

One of the Bible's most dramatic narratives is Genesis 22. God asked Abraham to sacrifice his only son, Isaac, whom he loved, as a burnt offering. The account develops at a slow pace. At the very beginning the biblical author informs the reader that it is a test and that by implication God will not allow Abraham to sacrifice Isaac. The Lord seeks to provide an occasion for Abraham to reveal the depth of his commitment to Him. A test is a means through which what is hidden or questioned makes itself present and visible to others. Why was it necessary for Abraham to reveal his faith, the nature of his commitment to God? The narrative itself does not provide an answer. In it we face only the painfulness and anguish of the test.

The fact that at the end of the experience God renews the covenant suggests that the test has a connection to the covenant that He made with Abraham. Earlier the Lord had said to him, "I am God Almighty; walk before me and be blameless. I will confirm my covenant between me and you and will greatly increase your numbers" (Gen. 17:1, 2). The divine promise was going to be fulfilled through his descendant, Isaac, born through Sarah (verse 16). He came as a gift from God, the result of a miraculous and divine intervention. But Abraham was not totally faithful to the covenant stipulations and did not walk "blameless" before the Lord. In that sense he violated the covenant. It was important for Abraham to manifest his faith, to reveal it in an unprecedented manner. Thus he found himself confronted with a test that must have shaken the core of his being.

It is not difficult to establish the nature of the test, and Abraham himself was most probably aware of it. The fundamental theological question behind it involved the important topic of the seed/descendant through whom God would fulfill the promise of salvation. Isaac, as the true seed, was a divine gift to Abraham and Sarah. But now the Lord was retrieving the gift—He wanted it back. No longer a true covenant partner, Abraham did not deserve it. In fact, the covenant was coming to an end and with it the election of the patriarch. Was Abraham willing to surrender the gift, or would he selfishly and rebelliously claim ownership of it? Would he be able to trust fully in the Lord and wait patiently in Him, believing that the Lord would be faithful to the promises He made to him in spite of his covenant breaking? He did, trusting God so much that he believed in the impossible—namely, in the resurrection of his son (Heb. 11:19).

The actual sacrifice did not take place, because God provided another sacrificial victim. The text simply says: "He went over and took the ram and sacrificed it as a burnt offering instead of his son" (Gen. 22:13). The reader can only imagine the deep emotions and feelings in the heart of the patriarch as he rushed over the rugged terrain to grab the ram in order to offer it to the Lord as a substitute for his only son. The burnt offering was an atoning sacrifice, and through it came forgiveness and covenant renewal (Gen. 22:15-18; cf. 8:20, 21; Lev. 1:3, 4).

The narrative combines a series of elements that will become important in the understanding of sacrificial atonement in the Bible. It brings together covenant breaking, divine abandonment, the possibility of death, a substitutive sacrifice, and the restoration of fellowship with God through covenant renewal. It is not strange to find some allusions to it in the New Testament in the context of the sacrificial role of Jesus. We will mention only some of them.

During the baptism of Jesus the voice of the Father is heard "from heaven" saying, "You are my Son, whom I love" (Mark 1:11). Genesis 22:2 describes Isaac not only as the son of Abraham but as the one "whom you love [Greek *agapētos*]." Jesus is the Son of God "whom I [the Father] love [*agapētos*]" (cf. John 3:16). The only place in the Old Testament in which anyone hears a voice from heaven is Genesis 22:15. Now the voice of the Father Himself addresses His Son from heaven. The salvific manifestation of the presence of God now occurs in the person of His beloved Son.

God said to Abraham, "You . . . have not withheld [LXX, *pheidomai*] your son, your only son" (verse 16). Paul writes, "He [God] who did not spare [*pheidomai*] his own Son, but gave him up for us all—how will he not also, along with him, graciously give us all things?" (Rom. 8:32). Both the Greek translation of the Old Testament and Paul used the same verb, *pheidomai* ("spare, refrain from something"). The parallel is in fact a contrast. Abraham's son was spared, but not God's Son. The experience of Abraham typified or pointed to Christ's actual sacrificial act.

Other references to Genesis 22 place the emphasis on the faith of Abraham, who trusted God to the point of being willing to sacrifice his son. Hebrews states that Abraham trusted God so much that he became persuaded that the Lord would resurrect Isaac from the dead in order to fulfill the promises He had made to him (Heb. 11:17-20). James uses the story to demonstrate that faith has to be accompanied by works of loving obedience to God (James 2:20-24). Biblical writers use the narrative to illustrate not only the sacrificial significance of the death of Christ but also the quality of the faith response of the believer to the God who provided the sacrifice for us.

The experience of Abraham in the Old Testament prefigured important elements of Christ's sacrificial death. It revealed some aspects of the redemptive plan of God for the human race. The Old Testament itself memorialized the incident: "And to this day it is said, 'On the mountain of the Lord it will be provided'" (Gen. 22:14). The reference is most probably to one of the most dramatic moments in the narrative, the moment that Isaac asked, "Where is the lamb?" and his father answered, "God himself will provide the lamb" (verses 7, 8). When his descendants went to worship on the mountain of the Lord, they also anticipated that ultimately the Lord Himself would supply the sacrificial victim for them.

The Servant of the Lord: Isaiah 52:13-53:12

As the Ethiopian eunuch read Isaiah 53 he became confused about the meaning of the text. When Philip approached him, he asked the apostle, "Tell me, please, who is the prophet talking about, himself or someone else?" (Acts 8:34).[6] Philip explained about Jesus in that passage and in other parts of the Bible. Isaiah 52:13-53:12 played a significant role in the ministry and teachings of Jesus as well as in the apostolic proclamation of His redemptive work. Through Isaiah the Lord preannounced the work of Christ to His people. That passage, written in Hebrew poetry, divides into five sections, or strophes.[7]

First section: Isaiah 52:13-15. The poem begins the way it ends, namely, with an exaltation of the Servant of the Lord (cf. Isa. 53:10-12), emphasizing the victory and success of His mission. The opening sentence is almost a shout of victory: "My servant will act wisely"—be successful—"he will be raised and lifted up and highly exalted" (Isa. 52:13; cf. Phil 2:9). The speaker seems to be God, who through the prophet announces that something unanticipated will happen. The poem commences with the reaction of the nations, who knew little or nothing about the work of God through His Servant (cf. Rom. 15:20, 21). At first the humiliating condition of the Servant appalled the "many nations." He looked like a human reject, disfigured and beyond human likeness (Isa. 52:14). But they will eventually be in silent awe, "for what they were not told, they will see, and what they have not heard, they will understand" (verse 15; cf. 1 Cor. 1:18, 25; Rom. 15:21).

Second section: Isaiah 53:1-3. The speaker is the "we," the people. This section begins with a rhetorical question addressed to those who knew about the coming of the Servant, but who did not recognize Him when He arrived. The prophet, representing the Lord, asks: "Who has believed our message . . . ?" (verse 1; cf. Rom. 10:16). Then follows the speech of the "we." They argued that when the Servant came they could not recognize Him because, first, He did not *look* like the Servant of the Lord—"he had no beauty or majesty to attract us to him, nothing . . . that we should desire him" (Isa. 53:2). Judged by His appearance, the Servant was the most unlikely candidate for that role. Second, He was also socially inadequate in that He was under great emotional pressure and suffering. They identified Him as "a man of sorrows" (verse 3), not as the Servant of the Lord. Consequently, humans "despised and rejected" Him (cf. Mark 9:12).

Throughout the poem we find several confessions from the group identified as the "we." The first one occurs in verse 3: "We esteemed [*chashab*] him not." The tone of the sentence is almost that of a lament and implies sorrow and repentance. In this context, the verb *chashab* means "to respect, to hold in high regard," even "to value" (e.g., Isa. 13:17; 33:8). Based on what they observed with respect to the experience and appearance of the Servant, they devalued Him by not being able to perceive in Him any divine redemptive significance.

Third section: Isaiah 53:4-6. Here the "we" describes the new understanding they have gained about the meaning of the experience of the Servant of the Lord. They realized that the Servant went through something that should have been theirs—that He "took up our infirmities and carried our sorrows" (verse 4; the Hebrew verb *nāśa'* means "to bear"; cf. Matt. 8:16, 17). Such a discovery placed their previous negative attitude toward Him in an even more painful light, thus forcing a second confession: "We considered him stricken by God, smitten by him, and afflicted" (Isa. 53:4). The admission acknowledges their wrong understanding of God's attitude toward the Servant. They thought they were on God's side when rejecting Him, and projected onto God their own feelings and attitudes toward the Servant. In a sense the sentence expresses a truth, namely, that God was indeed directly involved in what the Servant was experiencing; but the poem will deal with this later. It does not seem to be what the "we" had in mind, however.

The language used in the first part of Isaiah 53:4 introduced the concept of substitution by establishing a strong contrast between "we/our" and "He." He experienced—He bore—what was "ours." The condition of the Servant, which had diminished in their eyes His value, was precisely their own personal condition that He was removing from Him.[8] Verse 5 develops this thought much more when it declares that He was "pierced for our transgressions, he was crushed for our iniquities" (cf. Rom. 4:25). It is not that He participated in their condition, but that He suffered or took the ultimate result of their alienation from God upon Himself. The Servant assumed their place and received what was theirs, as the "we" explicitly expressed in the last part of verse 5, the third confession from the people: The "punishment that brought us peace was upon him," further explained as "by [Heb. b^e, "at the cost of"] his wounds we are healed" (cf.1 Peter 2:24). Here is their recognition that salvation came through the experience of the Servant. Because He took "our" *punishment,* "we" received from Him peace—His wounds brought healing to us.

The idea of substitution is even clearer in Isaiah 53:6. The verse begins with the fourth confession of the people. In the light of the saving work of the Servant the self-perception of the people radically changes. They acknowledge their need for salvation by comparing themselves with sheep that have gone astray—they all turn to their own ways (cf. Isa. 42:24; 48:17; 1 Peter 2:25). Now they have realized that what in fact happened was that "the Lord has laid on him the iniquity [Heb. *ʿawon,* "debt, guilt"] of us all" (cf. John 1:29). We see here the idea of a substitutive transfer of iniquity/guilt from the people to the Servant. It is how they were healed.

Fourth section: Isaiah 53:7-9. The speech of the people came to an end, and now we probably hear the voice of the Lord, as the phrase "my people" in verse 8 suggests. What we have is the Lord's perspective with respect to the experience of the Servant. It demonstrates that the people's new understanding of the work of the Servant was correct. Verse 7 describes Him as submissive. As He faced oppression and affliction, He did not open His mouth (cf. Matt. 26:63; 27:12, 14; 1 Peter 2:23). He was like a sheep going to the shearers, a lamb to the slaughter (cf. Acts 8:32, 33; Rev. 5:6, 12). Quietly He submitted to the divine *plan* for Him. Though He suffered an illegal execution, yet His descendants will

65

be numerous! The poem announces His redemptive death: "He was cut off from the land of the living; for the transgression of my people he was stricken" (Isa. 53:8; cf. 1 Cor. 15:3). His death was the result not of His sin, but of the sin of God's people, whose sin He had taken upon Himself. Because He had been executed as a criminal He should have been buried as one, but instead He was buried as a wealthy person. The passage explains the contrast by pointing to the fact that the Servant was totally innocent—He was a sinless person, free from violence and deceit (cf. 1 Peter 2:22; 1 John 3:5). Here we have the testimony of God Himself concerning His Servant.

Fifth section: Isaiah 53:10-12. The last strophe brings out the theological significance of the experience of the Servant. It completes the picture described in the previous verses by repeating and clarifying the role of God in the process and the full benefits of the mission of the Servant. What happened to Him was not an accident but the result of divine will. It was part of the divine plan that included crushing Him, causing Him to suffer. Scripture interprets that humiliating experience in terms of the Israelite sacrificial system. God offered Him as a guilt offering—an atoning sacrifice. Now all the language of suffering, disfigurement, wounds, punishment, and its association with transgressions and iniquities becomes clear. Treated as a sacrificial victim taking the sin of the people upon Himself, He died like a sacrificial victim—in place of the people.

But His death leads to resurrection: "He will see his offspring" (verse 10); "He will see the light of life and be satisfied" (verse 11). Back from the darkness of death, the Servant will continue to implement the will of the Lord—the redemptive plan. Its next aspect is the application of the benefits of His sacrificial death to those who believe: "By his knowledge my righteous servant will justify many, and he will bear their iniquities" (verse 11). The phrase "by his knowledge" could mean "as a result of his experience," that is to say, of His sacrificial death, or "by knowing" about Him, that is to say, by having a personal knowledge of or a faith relationship with Him. In God's redemptive purpose the two are inseparable. It is through that knowledge that the Servant declares the "many" righteous (cf. Rom. 5:19). The "many" are all those who, according to the poem, found in the suffering, death, and resurrection of the Servant a divine redemptive purpose for their lives. The declaration of righteousness is possible in that He bore their iniquities (verse 11).

The resurrection of the Servant also includes His exaltation (verse 12; cf. Isa. 52:13). The text gives as the reason for His exaltation that He was obedient even to the point of death. In doing that he was "numbered with the transgressors" (verse 12; cf. Luke 22:37). But it is not simply a case of sharing the fate of sinners. In fact, He "bore the sin of many" (Isa. 53:12; cf. Heb. 9:28; 1 Peter 2:24). Taking what belonged to the "many"—their sin—He bore it in their place.

He stood between God and the sinner as the intercessor for whom there was no intercessor. After His humiliation followed His exaltation (cf. 1 Peter 1:9, 10). We could also interpret the reference to His mediation in terms of what He would be doing for humans after His exaltation (cf. Rom. 8:34). In that case Isaiah 53:12 begins and ends with a reference to the exaltation of the Servant.

Isaiah 52:13-53:12 is an amazing prophecy of the future experience of the Messiah. The passage describes the Servant as a prophet (He is Himself a revelation of God), a king (through the use of the title Servant of the Lord and through His exaltation), and a priest (He intercedes for sinners). The poem of the Suffering Servant encapsulates in a powerful form the life, ministry, death, resurrection, exaltation, and mediation of Christ. It anticipated the atoning significance of His sacrificial death for sinners, whose sins He bore as their substitute. Centuries before the birth of Jesus, God was already announcing His plan for the human race.

The Coming Messiah: Daniel 9:23-27

Among the biblical books Daniel stands above all others as containing some of the most significant predictions related to the divine plan for the salvation of sinners. That plan would develop within human history and lead to the establishment of the kingdom of God on earth. This is particularly the case in Daniel 7-9, which outlines the conflict between evil powers, operating through political and religious systems, and the Son of Man, the Messiah, and His people.

The prophecy of Daniel 9:24-27 is especially important in that it predicts the moment of the arrival of the Messiah. It announces the coming of the Anointed One (Dan. 9:25), as well as His death (verse 26). His work would consist of establishing a firm covenant with many, bringing to an end the sacrifices (verse 27), finishing transgression, making atonement for iniquity, establishing everlasting righteousness, and inaugurating the sanctuary services (verse 24). Daniel predicts that all these events will take place within a period of 70 weeks (490 years), particularly toward the end of that period. With amazing precision it outlines the redemptive work of the coming Messiah.

Another amazing aspect of Daniel's prophecy is that it includes a point of departure for the initiation of the prophetic period. It would begin with the giving of a decree to "restore and rebuild" Jerusalem (verse 25). The book of Ezra (Ezra 7:11-26; 4:7-13) records such a decree, and we can date it to the seventh year of king Artaxerxes (Ezra 7:7), or 457 B.C. (by using the ancient fall-to-fall calendar [cf. Neh. 1:1; 2:1]). The prophetic period was segmented into seven weeks, 69 weeks (for the Anointed One to appear; A.D. 27), and the last, the seventieth week, divided into two halves. During the first half the Messiah would die (A.D. 31), bringing righteousness and atonement and establishing a firm covenant with many. The new covenant would lead to the second half of the week, when the faith of Israel would be universalized (A.D. 34; cf. Acts 7; 8:4, 5, 27-39; 9:31; 11:19; 28:28).

When we recall that this prophecy appeared hundreds of years before Christ, its fulfillment in the life and ministry of Jesus is simply impressive. His sacrificial death brought to an end the sacrificial system of the Old Testament by finding its fulfillment in Him (Matt. 27:51; Heb 10:8-10). Through His blood He established a new covenant that once and for all restored permanent fellowship with God (Heb. 8:6). His atoning sacrifice was and continues to be the only means for forgiveness of sin (1 John 1:9; 2:2; Eph. 1:7). Through Daniel God announced a series of vital aspects of the redemptive plan related to the coming Messiah, and they found their startling fulfillment in the person of the Son of God.

Conclusion

We have briefly examined some of the passages in the Old Testament in which the Lord announced the work of Christ to His people. He wanted them to understand that they had not been left alone under the power of sin and death and that a divine plan had been configured in the mystery of the Godhead to save them. The promise of salvation was specific enough for them to recognize its fulfillment. The prophetic Word slowly unveiled the mystery of atonement. Peter describes the process as follows: "Concerning this salvation, the prophets, who spoke of the grace that was to come to you, searched intently and with the greatest care, trying to find out the time and circumstances to which the Spirit of Christ in them was pointing when he predicted the sufferings of Christ and the glories that would follow. It was revealed to them that they were not serving themselves but you, when they spoke of the things that have now been told you by those who have preached the gospel to you by the Holy Spirit sent from heaven. Even angels long to look into these things" (1 Peter 1:10-12).

---

[1] See, Kenneth A. Matthews, *Genesis 1-11:26* (Nashville: Broadman and Holman, 1996), p. 245.

[2] T. S Desmond Alexander, "Messianic Ideology in the Book of Genesis," in *The Lord's Anointed: Interpretation of Old Testament Texts*, eds. Philip Satterthwaite, Richard S. Hess, and Gordon J. Wenham (Grand Rapids: Baker, 1995), p. 30.

[3] Walter Wifall ("Genesis 3:15—A Protevangelium?" *Catholic Biblical Quarterly* 36 [1974]: 361-365) has argued that Davidic and messianic ideology, as described in 2 Samuel 1-1 Kings 2, lies behind Genesis 3:15 as well as the ancient Near Eastern royal mythology, and concludes that the New Testament applies such a royal or messianic framework to Jesus. It is questionable that one could construct the background of Genesis 3:15 along those lines. However, it is important to observe the significance of the connection of a theological understanding of the "seed/descendants" with the dynasty of David.

[4] Douglas Moo, *The Epistle to the Romans* (Grand Rapids: Eerdmans, 1996), p. 933. See also C.E.B. Cranfield, *A Critical and Exegetical Commentary on the Epistle to the Romans* [Edinburgh: T. & T. Clark, 1979], vol. 2, p. 803), who goes even further and states, "That the promise refers to the eschatological consummation, and not to some special divine deliverance in the course of their [the Christians in Rome] lives, seems to us virtually certain."

[5] Walter Brueggemann, *Genesis* (Atlanta: John Knox, 1982), p. 50.

[6] Scholars still debate that question. The amount of literature written on the subject of that passage is enormous and reaches numerous and often contradictory conclusions. For an overview, see G. P. Hugenberger, "The Servant of the Lord in the 'Servant Songs' of Isaiah: A Second Moses Figure," in *The Lord's Anointed: Interpretation of Old Testament Messianic Texts*, pp. 101-139. We will approach the text from the perspective of the New Testament, which identifies the Servant of the Lord with Jesus Christ. The poem contains some textual problems and verses that are difficult to interpret. Reading several different translations will alert the reader to those difficulties. Space does not allow us to address them, however.

[7] John N. Oswalt, *The Book of Isaiah: Chapters 40-66* (Grand Rapids: Eerdmans, 1998), p. 376.

[8] *Ibid.*, p. 386.

6

THE ATONEMENT IN THE SHADOWS:
The Sacrificial System

It was daybreak in Babylon as the priests opened the doors of the temple. Soon they would offer the morning sacrifices, taking the meat inside the temple. Linen drapes provided privacy to the image of the god and to the table on which the priests placed the food. The sacrificial meat was the main dish and was accompanied by fruits and drinks. The priests were feeding the god. By having the food placed in front of the image and the drinks poured into cups before the cult image, the deity could assimilate the essence of the food. Then the priests removed the food that had been blessed through contact with the deity from the table and took it to the palace, where the king and his officers enjoyed it. The temple staff repeated the same ritual early in the evening. The obvious purpose of sacrifice was not to expiate sin, but to supply the needs of the gods. The people and the king enjoyed the favors of the gods by providing them with proper food.

But in the Bible God established the sacrificial system to illustrate how He would solve the problem of sin and strengthen and restore the covenant relationship between Him and the people. Consequently, it has played a significant role in the interpretation of the death of Jesus. Christians considered the system to have had a typological significance, pointing to the work of salvation of Christ for us and finding its fulfillment in Him. The sanctuary services revealed a way of ordering the world by establishing distinctions and boundaries that humans must respect in order to coexist in harmony with God and others. We should first examine in a general way that conceptual universe and then explore its significance.

Sanctuary Services and the Israelite Worldview

The worldview presupposed by the sanctuary services rests on the order established by God during Creation week. It also takes into consideration the disruption of that order through sin.[1] When we examine that perspective, we discover a web of concepts that shaped the way the Israelites were to relate to each other, to God, and to the rest of the world. Here we can provide only an incomplete and brief summary of that conceptual universe.[2] Within it the most important element in the lives of the Israelites was the presence of God in the sanctuary. The sanctuary was a space separated from the common for the Lord.[3] As a unique space it was accessible only to priests and Levites and, under certain circumstances, to the Israelites. Those who approached the Lord in His tabernacle had to take the utmost care. What made that space unique or holy was the fact that God had chosen to dwell there. In the biblical mentality any other space by nature lacked holiness. Holiness was of divine origin.

What, then, was the condition of the rest of the world? For the Israelites, whom God had separated from the nations, it was in a state of sin and separation from God, belonging to the common or profane, or in a condition of uncleanness/impurity (cf. Lev. 20:26).[4] The Lord created in the middle of the chaos of the profane, the unclean, and the sinful a Most Holy Place, making it possible for humans to approach Him, the source of life. Consequently, there were, so to speak, two spheres of existence. One was basically characterized by death and separation from God—the common, the sinful, and the unclean. The other had as its basic trait life and union to God—the holy and pure. God was the exclusive source of holiness. The sinful and the unclean also had a primary source. Leviticus 16 identified it as Azazel, whom we will argue was a demonic figure. This meant that the sanctuary services clearly depicted the cosmic conflict as a struggle between God and His people and the forces of evil.

Israelites conceived that, outside the sphere of holiness, the forces of sin and impurity had almost total control over the world. I say almost, because not everything was in a state of uncleanness. There were clean places (cf. Lev. 4:12; Num. 19:9), and there were clean animals that one could use for food and for sacrifices (Lev. 11). And the common was not necessarily evil, unless one treated the holy as something that was common, thus disrespecting and profaning it.[5] But ultimately every person or thing alive came under the power of the unclean, into the sphere of death. Death indeed reigned.

Was it possible for humans to move from the sphere of the unclean to that of the holy? Yes! Even those who were not descendants of Abraham could have that experience. Israel entered the sphere of the holy through God's election and through a covenant relationship with Him (cf. Deut. 7:6; 14:2, 21).[6] They, and anybody else interested in shifting from the one sphere to the other, had to go through certain transitional rituals in which sacrifices were of primary importance. The unclean was to be cleansed and purified, primarily through water, fire, or blood. The common was to be made holy, or allowed to participate of the holiness of the Lord, through sanctification rituals that employed blood and oil. And sin was to be removed through sacrificial blood and divine forgiveness. Such rites enabled humans to approach the Holy One in His holy dwelling. But holiness was more than a characteristic of a particular space.

The holy transformed those who approached the Lord and became a way of life that reflected His holiness—His divine character. Thus the holy contained an ethical dimension that distinguished it from the common and the unclean. Here the covenant became an intrinsic part of the religious life of the people of Israel. The covenant was the ethical expression of the holiness of God in their lives. By instructing the Israelites concerning how to relate to others and particularly to God, it created a barrier against the incursion of sin and impurity into the sphere of holiness. Therefore, any violation of the covenant was a serious threat both to the individual and to the community. Such violations placed the Israelites within the sphere of the common and the impure—the sinful—and thus ultimately under the power of the sphere of death.

Certain types of uncleanness were practically unavoidable for the Israelites, making the presence of the unclean inevitable within the covenant community. The biblical worldview also recognized that because of human frailty people could unintentionally sin. This suggests that the two spheres—of holiness and of uncleanness and sin—were not totally separated, but that to some extent they overlapped in complex ways.[7] Such phenomena revealed the conviction that human nature constantly needed cleansing and forgiveness in order to be able to exist in the presence of a Holy God. Here the sacrificial system became the vehicle that could daily free the individual from impurity and sin, particularly through the atoning rituals that the Lord used to establish, maintain, and restore order.[8]

Sin/Impurity and the Individual

As suggested above, the covenant relationship took moral and ritual violations very seriously. Violations of the ritual laws resulted in a state of impurity. In fact, we could say that impurity in the context of the sanctuary indicated a condition of alienation from God and other humans. An unclean person could not have contact with others and must not enter the sanctuary. Such individuals were in a sense removed from the sphere of fullness of life and considered to be within the influence and power of the sphere of death. Scripture identifies some specific sources of uncleanness, such as dead bodies (Num. 6:6, 7, 11), diseases (Lev. 13; 14), blood discharge, and semen (the "seed" of life). The list suggests that Israel fundamentally associated impurity with the sphere of death. A good illustration is the leper, considered to be in the sphere of death (Num. 12:9-12).

We can, then, suggest that the biblical worldview regarded the impure person to be in the realm of death, heading toward absolute alienation from the community and from the presence of the Lord within it. Obviously it was a very serious condition that required deliverance through the removal of the contaminant from the individual or the individual from the community. The Israelite sanctuary services made such deliverance possible through sacrificial atonement.

Moral faults are, in a sense, of a different nature, although the end result is basically the same: alienation from God. Here the emphasis is on sin as a burden and not as a *physical* contaminant. The result of sinning is a state of "guilt" (*'āshām*, Lev. 5:2), and the Old Testament describes the person as "bearing sin" (*nāsa' 'awôn*, verse 1). When the sinner is the subject of the phrase *nāsa' 'awôn* it means that the person is responsible for his or her sin and is liable to a punishment or penalty. The context identifies the penalty, and either the people or God inflict it (e.g., Lev. 20:20; 24:14, 15; Ex. 28:42, 43; Num. 9:13). The phrase "he/she bears sin" is a legal declaration indicating that a particular person is responsible for a specific sin and that a penalty—the consequence of the sin—is applicable. We find the idea of penalty also expressed by the verb *'āshām*, usually translated "to be guilty." It can refer to a sinful action (Ps. 68:21) as well as to the punishment for a wrongdoing—the consequences (Jer. 51:5; Gen. 26:10). In the context of the sanctuary services the tendency is to employ the consequential meaning of the verb, e.g., "to feel guilty," or to experience the consequences that resulted from the guilt of sin.[9] This includes ideas such as "become liable" (Lev. 4:3; 6:5, 7), and "experience liability" (Lev. 4:13, 27; 5:2-5, 17).[10]

Those who found themselves in a state of liability, bearing their own sin, needed immediate deliverance. Notice that in the context describing sinners as about to experience the full penalty for their sins they were allowed to bring a sacrifice to the Lord through which they freely received atonement and forgiveness of sin. The sacrificial victim played a significant role in their deliverance from the burden of sin or in the removal of their contamination. The ritual acts and Leviticus 17:11 help us to understand that role.

Blood and Atonement

Although the sacrificial system met a variety of needs, it had one fundamental function. Concerning the blood of the sacrificial victim, God said, "I have given it to you to make atonement for yourselves on the altar; it is the blood that makes atonement for one's life" (Lev. 17:11). A direct connection exists between the sacrifice, the use of blood, and the atoning process. The first thing we should notice is that atonement is a divine gift. God Himself provided the means and made it available to the Israelites. He gave them what they needed to restore their relationship with Him, namely, blood (verse 14; Gen. 9:4; Deut. 12:23).

Second, in Leviticus 17:11 text blood stands for life: "I have given it [the blood as life] to you to make atonement for yourselves [literally, for your life] on the altar; it is blood [as life] that makes atonement for [literally, in exchange for] one's life." The text addresses the fundamental issue of human life, but life that because of sin or impurity is endangered. In the atonement process the blood/life of the animal stands for the life of the individual, and God, as the proprietor of blood/life, receives the life of the animal as if it were the life of the repentant sinner. Thus the sanctuary system preserved human life at the cost of the life of the sacrificial victim.

Third, in Leviticus 17:11 the verb *kipper* ("to make atonement") expresses the idea of ransoming life.[11] The technical phrase "to make atonement for life" would then mean "to give a ransom for human life," implying that the blood/life of the sacrificial victim is the ransom offered to preserve human life. In this case, ransom and substitution are inseparable because the life of the victim stands in place of that of the guilty person.[12] This understanding of the verb is particularly valid when its object is a human being and applies not only to cases of moral faults but also to ritual contamination.[13] What we need to examine is how such an understanding of atonement expresses itself in the sacrifices.

Sacrifices and Atonement

The Israelite sanctuary services had two main atoning sacrifices, namely the "sin offering" (Lev. 4) and the "guilt offering" (Lev. 5:14-6:7). Additional sacrifices, although their main function was not atonement, also contained atoning elements. We will deal first with the atoning sacrifices.

Atoning sacrifices: the sin offering. We find the occasion for the "sin offering," or "purification offering," clearly stipulated in the text: "When anyone sins unintentionally and does what is forbidden in any of the Lord's commands" (Lev. 4:1). It had to do with unintentional moral faults. But the sanctuary system also required it when a person became ritually unclean. The cases listed indicate that in practically all situations the contamination was almost unavoidable (Lev. 12:1-8; 15:2, 13-16, 25-30). Israelites also brought the same type of sacrifice for intentional sin (Lev. 5:1-13). We are here referring to sins that were "*nondefiant* offenses rather than with flagrant, defiant violations"[14] for which there was not a means of atonement (Num. 15:30, 31). The procedure for the sacrifice depended on whose offering it was. When a layperson brought the sacrifice, the offerer laid hands on it, through which the person identified himself or herself with the victim to the point that whatever he or she was experiencing was now transferred to the victim (cf. Lev. 16:21; 4:29; cf. 7:18). The animal was slaughtered and a portion of the flesh ritually eaten by the priest (Lev. 6:26-30). In this way the priest bore the sin of the offerer on his own person as the representative of the Lord (Ex. 28:38). Some of the blood was placed on the horns of the altar of burnt offerings and the rest poured out at the base of the altar (Lev. 4:30). Blood/life belonged to the Lord, and through that ritual the Israelite returned it to Him. But, as we indicated, this blood/life was the ransom-substitute for the repentant sinner. By returning the life of the sinner in the form of the life of the sacrificial victim, the blood became a vehicle to transfer the sin/impurity to the sanctuary. Whenever the sacrifice was offered for the congregation or the priest, the transfer of sin was symbolically represented in a different way. In those cases the priest did not eat any of the flesh of the animal, because he could not bear his own sin. The blood was then taken inside the sanctuary, where the priest sprinkled some of it before the inner veil, placed some on the horns of the altar of incense, and poured out the rest at the base of the altar of burnt offerings (verses 5, 7).

Atoning sacrifices: the guilt offering. An Israelite brought the "guilt sacrifice," or "reparation offering," for several types of sins, and it required reparation, plus a 20 percent penalty, and a ram for atonement (Lev. 5:14-6:7). It was to be offered "when a person commits a violation and sins unintentionally in regard to any of the Lord's holy things" (Lev. 5:15)—cases in which someone desecrated the holy by accidentally misappropriating it. The person was not aware of the fact that it was God's property. Once the individual did become aware of the desecration, he was to restore the property to the Lord, add a compensation of 20 percent to it, and then bring the "guilt offering" to the priest, who was to "make atonement for him with the ram as a guilt offering, and he will be forgiven" (verse 16).

People also offered the "guilt offering" for suspected sin. Perhaps a person was going through a difficult experience and concluded that she or he had probably committed a sin against the Lord. Her conscience bothered her, but she was unable to identify a specific sin. In those cases God said to the Israelites to bring a "guilt offering" (verses 17-19). The Lord cared about the psychological well-being of His people and provided a way to restore peace to the human heart, even in cases in which a sin may not have been present at all. In this case God did not require restitution and compensation, because the individual only suspected that he or she had committed a sin.

Certain intentional sins also required the same type of sacrifice (Lev. 6:1-7). They included cases of misappropriation of property belonging to another person subsequently aggravated by a denial on the part of the culprit of the crime, who might even take an exculpatory oath before the Lord, desecrating His name. If the sinner did begin to feel guilty, he or she had to make restitution and compensation and to bring a ram for the "guilt offering." If repentance did occur and the person properly repaired the damage done, the Lord was always willing to provide a means of atonement.

The sacrificial procedure for the "guilt offering" differs from that of the "sin offering" only in the use of its blood (Lev. 7:1-7). In this case the priest tossed the blood/life of the sacrifice, which stood in place of the sinful life of the repentant sinner, on the sides of the altar of burnt offerings (verse 2). The blood ritual was simplified most probably because restitution and reparation, which in a sense attenuated the sinful act, preceded the sacrifice, making the expiatory function of the sacrifice less prominent.

Other sacrifices. Scripture records two other sacrifices whose primary function was not expiatory yet were also associated with atonement. The first one is the "burnt offering" (Lev. 1), in which the priest burnt the sacrificial victim in its entirety on the altar. Any Israelite could bring a burnt offering to the Lord as a voluntary act of worship (verse 2). The procedure included the laying of the hand on the head of the animal (verse 4), and tossing the blood on the sides of the altar of burnt offerings (verse 5). An Israelite brought the burnt offering in order to be accepted before the Lord (verses 3, 4), further defined as "to make atonement for him" (verse 4). The acceptance of the offering by God determined the acceptance of the presenter. It was, therefore, vital for the individual to bring a sacrificial victim without defect (Lev. 1:3; 22:22-25) and to perform the laying on of hands. Individuals also brought it as a votive or freewill offering (Lev. 22:17-19). The votive offering was an expression of gratitude to the Lord, and the freewill offering expressed personal devotion, thanksgiving, and joy. But since people always required forgiveness, it was also a means of expiation. The fact that the offering expressed different ideas explains why the blood manipulation was simplified. It indicates that even in cases in which a particular sin was not mentioned, the human heart was still in constant need of cleansing and forgiveness.

The "peace offering," or "well-being offering," was basically a voluntary sacrifice. We can subdivide it into three types, namely, a thanksgiving offering, a votive offering, and a freewill offering (Lev. 7:12, 15, 16). The offerer was to lay the hand on the head of the victim, slay it (verse 2), and have the priest toss the blood on the sides of the altar of burnt offerings (Lev. 3:2). The significant difference between the peace offering and the burnt offering is that here the priest gave the flesh of the victim back to the offerer for a communion meal with family and friends (Lev. 7:15; Deut. 12:17, 18). It suggests that the sacrificial act was a joyful occasion (cf. Gen. 31:54; 1 Sam. 11:14, 15; 1 Kings 8:62, 63) and that it served to strengthen the covenant relation through communion with God and other Israelites (cf. Deut. 27:7; 1 Kings 8:63). The breast of the victim and its right thigh went to the officiating priest (Lev. 7:32-34), who ate them with his family.

Leviticus does not explicitly assign atoning significance to the peace offering. But it did have some expiatory function, as suggested by the fact that the blood application was the same as for the burnt and guilt offerings. In addition, Ezekiel 45:15, 17 clearly states that the peace offering had an expiatory character (cf. Lev. 17:11). This sacrifice pointed to the fact that before God could accept the devotion and the expressions of gratitude and love of the Israelites, they needed to experience the cleansing power of sacrificial atonement. Since the atoning significance of this sacrifice was very limited, the people and the priest could eat the flesh of the animal in order to express communion with the Lord. *What removed sin was at the same time a means of communion with God.*

Typological Significance

Our previous analysis indicates, first, that the sacrificial system seemed to presuppose that the human heart is in constant need of cleansing. If God allowed humans to exist within the sphere of holiness it was not because they were holy, but because He granted them holiness as a gift and was ready to preserve and restore holiness to them on a daily basis. Human frailty manifested itself in committing involuntary sins and in some cases being unable to avoid ritual contamination. The Lord knew about that condition and made provision for it through sacrificial substitutive atonement. The human condition also manifested its distorted contours whenever individuals who, though deep in their hearts did not want to break away from the Lord, still committed sins. It was a disturbing existential dissonance that humans were unable to resolve. Again, the Lord provided a way to remove that condition by cleansing and forgiveness through a substitute. The sacrificial system indicated that God was ready to forgive any sin except an expression of arrogant rebellion against Him that involved permanently resisting His gracious offer of sacrificial atonement.

Second, the sacrificial system also revealed the seriousness of sin and God's reaction to it. Sin provoked His wrath by blocking the flow of His love toward the sinner. Those who were tainted by impurity and moral wrongs placed themselves in the sphere of death and separated themselves from the fullness of the purity and holiness of the Lord. They bore the responsibility and penalty of their sins. Without divine intervention they were heading toward permanent alienation from God—to death. But the Lord could through a substitute remove them from that sphere by cleansing and forgiving them. Even more than that, He did it by bearing their sins Himself: "The Lord, the Lord, the compassionate and gracious God, slow to anger, abounding in love and faithfulness, maintaining love to thousands, and forgiving wickedness [literally, "bearing the wickedness/penalty" (*nāsaʿ ʿawôn*)], rebellion and sin" (Ex. 34:6, 7). That divine loving disposition toward sinners manifested itself in the sacrificial system that symbolically represented the ultimate death of the sinner through the death of the sacrificial victim and whose sin/impurity was transferred to the very presence of God when the priest as His representative bore it for Him. It was as a result of that clash between sin/impurity and the holiness of God that atonement was possible, bringing cleansing and forgiveness for the repentant sinner.

Third, the Old Testament reveals that the sacrificial system had limitations. It was impossible for the sacrificial blood of animals to resolve the human problem. The Israelites knew that the problem of sin was so deeply rooted in the human heart that it would require God Himself to deal with it. So the psalmist prayed, "Have mercy on me, O God, according to your unfailing love; . . . blot out my transgressions. Wash away all my iniquity and cleanse me from my sin" (Ps. 51:1, 2). In a sense the psalm is saying that in order to be cleansed we have to rely on God's grace. The human problem is extremely serious: "Surely I was sinful at birth, sinful from the time my mother conceived me" (verse 5). Such a condition is not something that could be resolved through sacrificial offerings. Therefore, the psalm appeals to God Himself for forgiveness, recognizing that cleansing power was indeed located in the Lord.

Leviticus 4:26 also suggests the recognition that the sacrificial services were insufficient in and of themselves: "In this way the priest will make atonement for the man's sin, and he will be forgiven." Even after the performance of the rite of atonement, forgiveness was not automatic. The passive verb translated as "he will be forgiven" is a "divine passive," and it implies that the One who is granting the forgiveness is God Himself. We can then suggest that the ritual itself had a symbolic value and served to act out the feelings and experiences of the worshipper and to visualize the costliness of forgiveness and to prefigure the final resolution to the human predicament.

The fact that within the ritual acts Scripture describes the priest as bearing the sins of the people may also suggest that in the final analysis that cleansing and forgiveness could not come through the blood of an animal. Humanity needed a human mediator before God who could bear the responsibility and penalty for sin. Yes, the sacrificial victim bore the sin of the repentant Israelite and its blood ransomed/substituted for his or her life, but something of more value was required. We see this concept symbolically represented in the act of the priest bearing the sins of the people. The "something of more value" was what the Servant of the Lord was going to offer to the human race, namely, His own life as a "guilt offering" for the sins of many. As we saw, He was to bear the sins of many and to intercede for them. At this point the announcement of the coming Messiah in Isaiah and Daniel, and the typological significance of the sacrificial system, merge into each other, proclaiming in the Old Testament God's future salvific intervention in the person of His Son.

Conclusion

God announced His plan for the redemption for the human race through the sanctuary services. The sacrificial system became a study book for the Israelites concerning the way the covenant Lord was dealing with the alienating power of sin and uncleanness, and signalized His final resolution. Under the shadows of the sacrifices they heard the loving will of God proclaiming the provision of an abundance of grace of such magnitude that it will resolve once and for all the invasion of sin in the human heart and in the world. The sphere of holiness that God had created within Israel would in the future encompass the totality of the earth, filling it with His glory. It would occur not through the blood of animals, but through the sacrificial death of His Servant, who was prefigured in the shadows of the substitutionary death of a sacrificial victim. Through Him, God Himself would bear the sins of the world.

---

[1] Cf. Frank H. Gorman, Jr., *The Ideology of Ritual: Space, Time and Status in the Priestly Theology* (Sheffield: Sheffield Academic Press, 1990), pp. 39-45.

[2] For a moral technical analysis, see Philip Peter Jenson, *Graded Holiness: A Key to the Priestly Conception of the World* (Sheffield: Sheffield Academic Press, 1992); and Gorman, pp. 39-60.

[3] See Saul M. Olyan, *Rites and Ranks: Hierarchy in Biblical Representations of Cult* (Princeton, N.J.: Princeton University Press, 2000), p. 16.

[4] Jenson (p. 47) suggested that the clean "embraces the normal state of human existence in the earthly realm." This is true of the Israelites, but from their perspective it was hardly true of the nations who did not know the laws of holiness. The distinction between Israel and the nations was to a certain extent represented through the significance of the food laws. David P. Wright stated, "Just as God has separated the people from the nations, so the people are to make a separation between pure and impure animals. The diet thus encodes the social and political situation of Israel among the nations" ("Holiness in Leviticus and Beyond," *Interpretation* 53, no. 4 [1999]: 353, 354).

[5] The common was in principle the sphere that mediated or facilitated movement toward the unclean or, in the opposite direction, toward the clean and holy. Within Israel the common was not necessarily a negative condition. Legal as well as illegal profanation existed. For instance, a legal or legitimate profanation of the holy took place through the redemption of the firstborn of humans and of the unclean animals (Ex. 13:2, 12-15; Num. 18:15-18). An illegitimate profanation would be a serious matter, as would be the case, for instance, of profaning the name of God (Lev. 20:3), and the Sabbath (Ex. 31:14). See Olyan, pp. 26, 27; Wright, pp. 352, 360.

[6] See Wright, p. 353.

[7] Jenson, p. 49.

[8] Gorman, p. 52.

[9] Jay Sklar, *Sin, Impurity, Sacrifice, Atonement: The Priestly Conceptions* (Sheffield: Sheffield Phoenix Press, 2005), pp. 39-41.

[10] Roy Gane, *Leviticus and Numbers: The New International Version Application Commentary* (Grand Rapids: Zondervan, 2004), pp. 120, 121.

[11] See Jacob Milgrom, *Leviticus 17-22* (New York: Doubleday, 2000), p. 1474.

[12] See William K. Gilders, *Blood Ritual in the Hebrew Bible: Meaning and Power* (Baltimore: Johns Hopkins University Press, 2004), p. 176.

[13] Gane, p. 305; Sklar, pp. 154-159.

[14] Gane, p. 123.

7

THE ATONEMENT IN THE SHADOWS:
Day of Atonement

During the spring the Babylonians celebrated the festival of the new year. As part of the celebrations the priests of its gods would purify their temples. On the fifth day of the feast, very early in the morning, a priest washed himself and dressed in a linen robe. He went into the temple with a censer, a torch, and a sacred vessel to purify the building. Having brought with him water from the Tigris and Euphrates rivers, he sprinkled it on the sanctuary and placed cedar oil on the doors of the temple. A ram was slaughtered, and a priest performed the cleansing of the temple by taking the flesh of the animal inside the temple and walking around while lifting it up. Then he left the temple, went to the river, and threw the carcass of the animal into the water.

The Babylonians purified their temples from the presence of demons. They believed that demons liked to inhabit the temples of the gods. If the priests did not remove them, the gods would abandon the temples and the people. In Israel the situation was totally different. Its sanctuary was cleansed once a year from the sins and impurities of the people of Israel that had been transferred there through the daily sacrifices (Lev. 16). The ritual symbolically represented the time that God, from His heavenly dwelling place, will bring to an end the problem of sin, restoring the whole universe to the harmony that characterized it when God originally created it.

Summary of the Ritual

We will briefly mention some of the main elements of the complex ritual for the Day of Atonement. In preparation for the cleansing of the tabernacle, the high priest had to undergo a ritual bath and dress like a regular priest (Lev. 16:4). He had to bring a bull for a sin offering and a ram for a burnt offering. The people were to bring to him two male goats for a sin offering and a ram for a burnt offering. Then he cast lots on the two goats provided by the people to select one for the Lord as a sin offering, and the other for Azazel (verses 7, 8). The high priest offered the bull for his sin offering to make atonement for himself and his household, took fire and burned incense in the Most Holy Place, and sprinkled some blood once on the mercy seat and seven times in front of it (verses 11-14). Next the high priest moved to the holy place, put some blood around the horns of the altar of incense, and sprinkled seven times in front of it.[1] He was to do the same with blood of the goat for a sin offering for the people (verse 15). In this way he made atonement for the Most Holy Place. Finally, the high priest mixed the blood of both the bull and the goat and used it to make atonement of the altar of burnt offerings. Some of the blood he placed around the horns of the altar and some he sprinkled seven times on it to consecrate it (verses 18, 19).

Once he had completed the work of atonement in the tabernacle, the high priest approached the live goat brought by the people upon which the lot for Azazel had fallen. He placed both hands on it, confessed on it all the sins of the people of Israel—transferring them to it—and sent the goat into the wilderness (verses 20, 21). It bore all the iniquities of the people to a solitary land (verse 22).

Purpose of the Ritual

The Day of Atonement ceremony purified the tabernacle from "the uncleanness and rebellion of the Israelites, whatever their sins have been" (verse 16). The high priest applied the blood to the altar of burnt offerings "to cleanse it and to consecrate it from the uncleanness of the Israelites" (verse 19). Impurity and sin reached the sanctuary through the sacrificial offerings brought throughout the year by the Israelites. Such "contamination" was not something forced on God or on His dwelling, but something He willed to happen. As we already saw, He gave to the Israelites the blood of the sacrifices to make atonement for their lives on the altar (Lev. 17:11). God was telling His people, "If you have committed a sin or have become unclean, bring that impurity or sin to Me, and I will remove it from you by transferring it to My dwelling place."

On the Day of Atonement the Lord cleansed the sanctuary from the sins atoned for and from the uncleanness removed from the Israelites. During that day the work of atonement in Israel reached unanticipated dimensions. The purpose of the ritual was not to forgive the sins of the Israelites. Atonement was made for (*kipper 'eth*) the Most Holy Place, the holy place, and the altar (Lev. 16:33). But such atonement was made *for the benefit of* (*kipper 'al*) the people (verse 33). The object of atonement (indicated in Hebrew by the particle *'eth*), is nonpersonal, that is to say, it is the sanctuary and the altar. In that case the verb *kipper* expresses the idea of removing or cleansing. At the same time that cleansing of the holy objects benefited the people. During the Day of Atonement their forgiveness and cleansing reached its consummation. The problem of sin and impurity was fully addressed only when they were removed from the dwelling of the Lord. It was not a matter of forgiving the sinner, because any Israelite had already received forgiveness whenever he or she brought a sacrifice. By the cleansing of the holy objects from the sins of the people, an all-encompassing event took place that benefited them: "Then, before the Lord, you will be clean from all your sins" (verse 30). The statement has an element of finality about it. The sins committed during that year, the imprint they left on the tabernacle, were now *deleted* forever. No record of them remained!

The Day of Atonement reaffirms the fact that in the sanctuary services atonement was a process. Scripture does not restrict the use of the Hebrew verb *kipper* ("to make atonement") in the Israelite sacrificial system to one specific element of the rituals. The Old Testament associates it with the sacrificial victim (Lev. 1:4), the use of the fat and blood in the rituals (Lev. 4), the eating of the flesh of the sacrificial victim by the priest (Lev. 10:17), the sprinkling of the blood (Lev. 16:15, 16), the use of the blood on the altar (Lev. 17:11), and with the ritual as a whole (Lev. 5:6, 10; 10:1-9). Atonement was the result of the totality of the sacrificial system that included the slaying of the victim and the ministry of the priest on behalf of repentant sinners. But the Day of Atonement indicates that atonement also included the cleansing activities—that is to say, the consummation on the Day of Atonement of the daily atoning activities on behalf of the people.[2]

Role of Azazel

Possibly the most intriguing element in the ritual of purification of the sanctuary is the presence of the goat for Azazel. Some Bible versions translate "Azazel" as "scapegoat," but such a rendering is far from certain. Scholars have proposed several explanations of that name, but we still do not know the exact root meaning of the word. In a sense, it is not necessarily important to know its root meaning as long as we are able to identify its function during the Day of Atonement. When we examine the text, several things are relatively clear.

First, the figure of Azazel appears in the text once the cleansing of the sanctuary was completed: "When Aaron has finished [*killāh*] making atonement for the Most Holy Place, the Tent of Meeting and the altar, he shall bring forward the live goat" (Lev. 16:20). As indicated, the cleansing of the sanctuary brought with it some benefits for the Israelites. The Hebrew term *killāh* means "to complete," "to bring to an end," indicating that whatever the goat was going to accomplish, it did not make any contribution to the cleansing of the tabernacle itself. The impurities and sins of the people had already been removed from there.

Second, Azazel stands in contrast to Yahweh. There were two goats, and lots were cast in order to select one "for [l^e] Yahweh" and the other "for [l^e] Azazel" (see verse 8). The preposition "for" (Heb. l^e) means "belonging to," suggesting that one will be used in the service of the Lord and the other in that of Azazel. We are dealing here with personal names and therefore with persons. The first goat is not the Lord and neither is the other goat Azazel, but their respective roles are connected with those two figures. In fact, the goat could not be Azazel, because it was sent to Azazel (see verse 10).

Third, Azazel exists outside the Israelite camp, in the wilderness. The second goat was to be sent "to Azazel," to the "wilderness" (Heb. *midbār*) (verse 10). The Bible employs *midbār* in different ways, but it particularly stands for land hostile to human life (e.g., Num. 20:5; Ps. 107:4, 5; Jer. 2:6), desolate (e.g., Jer. 4:26), and inhabited by wild animals (Deut. 8:15). From there the enemy and other forces of chaos threaten to invade and upset organized social life (e.g., Jer. 5:6; 12:12; 13:24). It is also a place for demons (e.g., Isa. 13:19-22; Rev. 18:2; Isa. 34:14). Azazel dwelt in the wilderness, in a land characterized by chaos and the absence of fullness of life. He has been correctly identified as a demonic power.[3]

Fourth, the goat for Azazel functioned as a means of transportation. On it the high priest placed and sent to Azazel "all the iniquities of the children of Israel, and all their transgressions in all their sins" (Lev 16:21, KJV). This is what scholars call an elimination rite, something quite common throughout the ancient Near East. Such rituals sought to return to the gods or demons the evil that was afflicting a person, a city, or an army. The animal or object carried the evil away, and the intention was to return it to its place of origin. Azazel belonged to the sphere of death and chaos, and the load of sin was sent back to him as the source of its ultimate origin.[4] It suggests that Israel did not conceive of sin and impurity as demonic manifestations, but rather as demonic in origin.

Fifth, in a sense the goat for Azazel was involved in the cleansing. The text says: "But the goat chosen by lot as the scapegoat shall be presented alive before the Lord to be used for making atonement by sending it into the desert as a scapegoat" (verse 10). It does not mean that the sins and impurities of the people are atoned for through Azazel. God atoned them through the daily services and through the goat for the Lord during the Day of Atonement. Atonement is made upon the goat for Azazel in the sense that by placing the sins of the people on it to send them to Azazel, he is identified as the source of sin and impurity (cf. verses 21, 22).[5]

Meaning of the Ritual

Elements of the meaning of the ritual have already appeared in the previous discussion, but we need to develop them further and explore additional ideas.

Although Leviticus 16 is the only place that specifically discusses the ritual, its theological content surfaces in other parts of Scripture.

All-encompassing cleansing. We need to examine the all-encompassing nature of the cleansing accomplished during the Day of Atonement. The fact that once a year the tabernacle and the altar were totally cleansed suggests that we must not conceive of sin and impurity as having a permanent existence. Since for a short period of time they ceased to be present, one could conclude that they were considered to be by nature transient and, consequently, that one could permanently extinguish them. The Day of Atonement was perhaps a foretaste of a future perpetually free from the presence of sin and impurity in the camp of Israel. As long as it was repeated year after year, it was clear that the final resolution of the problem of sin/impurity was not yet a reality. But the yearly repetition of the ritual was in a sense a typological representation that anticipated the final eradication. We find some support for this in the proclamation of the jubilee during the Day of Atonement.

The jubilee introduced a new beginning in the life of the Israelites and became in the Old Testament "an eschatological hope of God's final restoration of humanity and nature to his original purpose." Therefore, the Day of Atonement was not simply the reenactment of a past condition, a momentary return to the original paradisiacal conditions after Creation, but the anticipation of a future event that would permanently reestablish that original condition. We have uncovered here an eschatological concern within the sanctuary services.

The Old Testament prophets echo this all-encompassing cleansing in the context of the restoration of the people of God. Through Isaiah the Lord proclaimed, "I have swept away your offenses like a cloud, your sins like the morning mist. Return to me, for I have redeemed you" (Isa. 44:22; cf. Ps. 103:12). It was the announcement of a new beginning for the people of Israel of the same quality as that anticipated in the ritual of the Day of Atonement. Both pointed to a future free from the problem of sin. Ezekiel proclaimed the coming of a time that "the people of Israel will no longer stray from me, nor will they defile themselves anymore with all their sins. They will be my people, and I will be their God" (Eze. 14:11). The prophet announced the coming of what the Day of Atonement anticipated—namely, that the incursion of sin among God's people will at last end. After returning from the exile, "they will no longer defile themselves with their idols and vile images or with any of their offenses, for I will save them from all their sinful backsliding, and I will cleanse them. They will be my people, and I will be their God" (Eze. 37:23; cf. Micah 7:18). It was to be the permanent realization of the final extirpation of sin ritually expressed during the Day of Atonement.

In the book of Daniel the Messiah is the one who brings to an end the sin problem. He will come "to finish the transgression, and to make an end of sins, and to make reconciliation for iniquity, and to bring in everlasting righteousness" (Dan. 9:24, KJV). The event depicted has a cosmic significance and points to the ultimate cleansing from sin. This is particularly the case in Daniel 8, in which the ideology of the Day of Atonement plays a central role. In that chapter we find a reference to the priestly work of the Prince of the heavenly hosts during the daily services in the heavenly temple and to the opposition to it by the little horn (Dan. 8:11). Then the vision shifts to the moment that the temple of God will be restored to its original order through a cosmic cleansing (verse 14). Such a cleansing brings with it the final defeat of the enemies of the Lord. The prophet employs the imagery and theology of the Day of Atonement to announce the eschatological liberation of the cosmos from the miasma of sin and impurity. Similarly Hebrews 9:23 speaks of the future aspect of the priestly work of Christ for His people in the heavenly tabernacle. In Jewish apocalyptic writings "the annual Yom Kippur was perceived—at least by some—as a ritual anticipation of the eschatological purification of God's creation from sin."[6]

Ultimate cleansing vindicates the people. The Day of Atonement reaffirms the acceptance of the people before the Lord. The ritual presupposed that God had cleansed and forgiven His people through the sin and guilt offerings and that their covenant relationship with Him had remained intact. During that day a spirit of submission to and trust in the Lord made this spiritual dimension of the people patently clear. They were not adding anything new to their spiritual condition, but revealing what was already there. A judicial procedure disclosed the quality of their spiritual life. The Day of Atonement was a day of judgment in Israel.

God's involvement in the problem of the sin and impurity of His people made necessary an examination of their spiritual condition. He had cleansed and forgiven them, but the question remained: Had they taken full advantage of the gift of divine grace, or had they broken away from the Lord? The judicial nature of the Day of Atonement acknowledged that some of those who benefited from the forgiving and cleansing grace of the Lord may have afterward abandoned Him. Divine justice demanded that such individuals should not be allowed to benefit from the all-encompassing cleansing offered to them during the Day of Atonement. In order for such a decision to be reliable, though, it was grounded on the legal basis provided by the divine judgment.

The Lord clearly stipulated the criteria employed in the legal investigation: "On the tenth day of the seventh month you must deny yourselves and not do any work—whether native-born or an alien living among you—because on this day atonement will be made for you, to cleanse you" (Lev. 16:29, 30). The Lord sought to find among His people total reliance on Him at the moment when ultimate cleansing was about to happen (cf. Deut. 8:2). The verb "to deny oneself" probably included different expressions of humility, but it certainly involved fasting (e.g., Isa. 58:3, 5). Fasting shifted the preservation of life away from the hand of the individual and placed it in the hands of the Lord. It was total reliance on the sustaining and preserving power of God (cf. Ezra 8:21). The rest required from the people was of the same type as that of the weekly Sabbath. That day they were to perform no work at all. Productivity that contributed to self-preservation was forbidden. By abstaining from such things they outwardly expressed their full commitment to the Lord, who freely cleansed and forgave them through the sacrificial system.

Those who demonstrated total dependence on the cleansing power of the Lord received the fullness of the cleansing offered to them as a gift during the Day of Atonement. However, those found to be self-reliant and rebellious were expelled from the community. In fact, the Lord Himself participated in the executive phase of the judgment: "Anyone who does not deny himself on that day must be cut off from his people. I will destroy from among his people anyone who does any work on that day" (Lev. 23:29, 30). God did not make His decisions concerning the future of the individual and the community arbitrarily. Grounding them on a legal basis upheld the justice of the decisions, and the people themselves were vindicated in the sense that their ultimate cleansing was seen to be an expression of their total dependence on the Lord.

The idea of God establishing distinctions among the people through divine judgment has eschatological dimensions in the Scriptures. Ezekiel announces that the return to the land will accompany a work of judgment through which, the Lord declares, "I will purge out from among you the rebels, and them that transgress against me: I will bring them forth out of the country where they sojourn, and they shall not enter into the land of Israel: and ye shall know that I *am* the Lord" (Eze. 20:38, KJV). Jesus in His parables pointed to the eschatological moment when the divine Judge will separate from among His people the faithful from unfaithful (Matt. 13:24-30, 47-50). The image of the eschatological harvest provides a cosmic dimension for that division. We see this particularly in Joel 3:11-13, in which the nations of the earth come before the judge of the earth, and Revelation 14:14-20, which describes the universal harvest. It is appropriate to conclude that the Day of Atonement was the ritual expression of that most important eschatological judgment that will lead into a new beginning of harmony and peace.

Cultic theodicy.[7] The word "theodicy" derives from the Greek *theos* ("God") and *dike* ("justice"), and is used to indicate that God is just in spite of the presence of evil in the world. The Day of Atonement served to justify the way that God had dealt with the problem of sin and impurity in Israel, as indicated in several ways in the ritual. First, as we have already mentioned, the presence of the concept of judgment in the ritual suggests that we are dealing with a theodicy. A judgment seeks to uncover the truth in situations in which it is not obviously accessible to the common observer. During that day God functioned as judge in order to demonstrate that the way He dealt with the sin/impurity of the people was legally justifiable and not an arbitrary decision on His part. He gave to each one what they legally deserved.

Second, the removal of sin/impurity from God's dwelling place revealed that He did not have anything in common with it. Consequently, it was impossible for them to coexist permanently within the camp. The Day of Atonement reaffirmed the fact that when the Lord assumed responsibility for sin/impurity in the tabernacle, He was bearing it as a manifestation of His forgiving grace and not because somehow He was directly and naturally connected to it (e.g., Ex. 34:7). His rendezvous with sin/impurity had a saving purpose and nothing else. The ritual of the Day of Atonement graphically illustrated the incompatibility between holiness and sin/impurity by removing the latter from the tabernacle, out of the camp, and finally by sending it away into the wilderness.

Third, the removal of sin/impurity from God's tabernacle indicated that holiness was superior to sin/impurity. Here was indeed a message of hope. Not even in the act of forgiving and cleansing His people did God get tainted by sin/impurity. Yes, in the atonement sin/impurity and holiness touched each other, but God's holiness remained absolutely undamaged, and He amazingly was able to restore holiness to His people. We see that superiority ritually manifested during the sanctuary services when the sacrificial victim bore sin/impurity but its flesh remained most holy. The same phenomenon is also present in the case of the priest, who, after eating of the flesh of the sin offering, now bore the sins of the people and yet remained holy. The Day of Atonement clarified the nature of the connection between sin/uncleanness and the Holy One.

Fourth, by removing sin/impurity from the tabernacle, God ritually proclaimed His power and sovereignty over evil powers. Azazel was simply impotent to oppose the divine work during the Day of Atonement. His silence was that of the accused, who, when confronted with the evidence against him or her, was left speechless, totally unable to rebut it. The goat carried the sin of the people to Azazel in submission to God and under the guidance of an instrument appointed by Him. One could even say that the inactivity of Azazel was an acknowledgement of guilt. In this powerful display of His sovereignty, God was simply restoring things to the original order established by Him. Creation through separation found its counterpart in God's work of re-creation through another act of separation.

Fifth, removing sin/impurity from the tabernacle during the Day of

Atonement pointed to Azazel as its originator and ultimate source. God's dwelling place among the Israelites established a strong connection between Him and their sin/impurity, particularly when He decided to assume responsibility for their sin/impurity by allowing it to be shifted to His holy sanctuary—moving it from the repentant sinner into it. In fact, transferring that miasma to His dwelling could have easily given His people the impression that they were sending it back to its place of origin through the sacrificial victim and the work of the high priest. But the elimination rite prevented such a misconception. The cultic theodicy was particularly present in the elimination rite for Azazel.

It is indeed amazing that the ritual of the Day of Atonement unexpectedly introduces the figure of Azazel. The reason? As already indicated, it clarified that sin/impurity originated not in the Lord but in the sphere of chaos and death. Thus it fully exonerated God from any potential charges against the integrity of His character based on the presence of sin/impurity within His creation. This is a theodicy par excellence and is fully compatible with the biblical view of a cosmic conflict between God and evil forces. The figure of Azazel clarified that a power inferior to the Lord constantly attempted to upset the divine order while God constantly sought to preserve or restore it. The Day of Atonement proclaimed that God will ultimately be victorious.

Conclusion

The Day of Atonement was the climactic moment in Israel's sanctuary services. The intricacy of the ritual reveals the complexity involved in the final resolution of the sin/impurity problem. Its eschatological significance expressed in ritual form the prophetic announcement of a future for the people of God free from the presence of sin through an act of divine re-creation. In both cases judgment and theodicy came to play central roles in the future resolution of the presence of sin/impurity within God's creation. A spirit of total submission and dependence on His power over sin and evil powers among God's people was to accompany the divine saving work.

---

[1] This is not explicitly stated in Leviticus 16, but verse 16 indicates that Aaron was to cleanse the holy place, and Exodus 30:10 makes clear that once a year atonement was to be made for the altar of incense (see Roy Gane, *Cult and Character: Purification Offerings, Day of Atonement, and Theology* [Winona Lake, Ind.: Eisenbrauns, 2005], pp. 226-230).

[2] See, R. J. Thompson, "Sacrifice and Offering: I. Old Testament," in *New Bible Dictionary*, eds. J. D. Douglas, F. F. Bruce, J. I. Packer, N. Hillyer, D. Guthrie, A. R. Millard, and D. J. Wiseman (Wheaton, Ill.: InterVarsity, 1982), p. 1052. He alerts us "against confining the atonement to a single act, as if it were the death alone, or the presentation of the blood, or the disposal of the victim, which atoned."

[3] See, among many others, David P. Wright, "Azazel," in *Anchor Bible Dictionary*, vol. 1, p. 536.

[4] Daniel Stökl comments, "The goat originally sent *to* Az'azel was seen [in the Jewish apocalytic literature] as the personification *of* Az'azel, the demonic source of sin *himself*" ("Yom Kippur in the Apocalyptic *Imaginaire* and the Roots of Jesus' High Priesthood," in *Transformation of the Inner Self in Ancient Religions*, eds. Jan Assmann and Guy G. Stroumsa [Leiden: Brill, 1999], p. 356).

[5] Gane, *Cult and Character*, pp. 261, 262.

[6] Christopher J. H. Wright, "Jubilee, Year of," in *Anchor Bible Dictionary*, vol. 3, p. 1029.

[7] Stökl, p. 356.

[8] Gane (*Cult and Character*, pp. 305-354) provides the best full treatment of the Day of Atonement as a theodicy.

8

ATONEMENT AND THE
Incarnation

As we begin to examine the biblical understanding of the incarnation of the Son of God we must acknowledge His preexistence. The incarnation is the enfleshment not of an idea but of a person. That by itself indicates that such an individual had a prior existence and that now that existence had taken on a new expression. This fact is of fundamental importance when dealing with the incarnation of Christ. In other words, in order for us to be able to talk meaningfully about the incarnation of the Son of God, we have to presuppose that He existed prior to His incarnation. And we find abundant biblical support for such an idea.

Evidence for the Preexistence of the Son of God

He was the Creator. Possibly the most important statements about the preexistence of Christ are those that identify Him as the means of creation. Paul speaks of Him as the Lord, "through whom all things came" (1 Cor. 8:6), and adds that "by him all things were created: things in heaven and on earth, visible and invisible, whether thrones or powers or rulers or authorities; all things were created by him and for him" (Col. 1:16). Hebrews uses more explicit cosmic language by identifying the Son of God as the one who "made the universe" (Heb. 1:2; cf. verse 10). Possibly John gives the most penetrating description of the creative power of the Son of God: "Through him all things were made; without him nothing was made that has been made" (John 1:3). He was God's instrument of creation in all of its expressions. John rules out the idea that the Son was the first act of divine creation. Since He made everything that ever came into existence, He is self-existent. Prior to the creation of the universe, He was.

He was active in the history of Israel. The New Testament establishes a direct relation between Christ and His people during the period of the Old Testament. Paul identifies the rock that followed the Israelites as Christ (1 Cor. 10:4). Not only was there a natural rock from which water flowed (Ex. 17:6;

Num. 20:11), but also a "spiritual rock" (1 Cor. 10:4). The reference is to several passages in Deuteronomy that identify God as the Rock (Deut. 32:4) and Savior (verse 15), the Creator of the people of Israel (verse 18), and the Rock that was in charge of them (verses 30, 31). The Rock that created Israel and guided the people throughout the wilderness was Christ. It was He that the people tested, and as a result many perished from the snakes (1 Cor. 10:9). Christ was also active in the revelation and inspiration of the Old Testament prophets. To them God revealed the future salvation that Christ would accomplish. They tried "to find out the time and circumstances to which the Spirit of Christ in them was pointing when he predicted the sufferings of Christ and the glories that would follow" (1 Peter 1:11). Although the phrase "Spirit of Christ" lends itself to different interpretations (e.g., the Spirit that announced the Messiah or the Spirit later revealed in Jesus), the use of similar phrases in the New Testament suggests that the Spirit is the One sent by Christ and that it testifies about Him (Rom. 8:9; Acts 16:7; Gal. 4:6; Phil. 1:19). The implication is that, since Christ sent to them the Spirit that inspired the Old Testament prophets, Christ was actively involved in the work of revelation during that same period, thus affirming His preexistence. The idea is not strange to Peter, who, after stating that the Godhead had chosen Christ before the foundation of the world to be the sacrificial lamb, adds that He has been "revealed in these last times for your sake" (1 Peter 1:20). Since the one who is revealed is Christ Himself, not an impersonal divine plan, a proper reading of the text demands His preexistence.[1]

He descended/came. The Bible describes the presence of Jesus among us as a descent and a coming, suggesting that He was somewhere else before being here (cf. John 3:13, 31). He descended from heaven with a very specific mission, and He fulfilled it (John 6:38). We find that such language refers to His origin supported by the fact that the Jews who heard Him asked themselves, "Is this not Jesus, the son of Joseph, whose father and mother we know? How can he now say, 'I came down [*katabainō*, "to descend"] from heaven'?" (verse 42). In a statement that anticipated His ascension, Jesus explicitly indicated His place of origin: "What if you see the Son of Man ascend to where he was before!" (verse 62). An ascent would follow the descent.

We also find Jesus saying "I have come . . ." in contexts that presuppose His preexistence.[2] An infinitive of purpose commonly follows that formula, indicating that the coming was a deliberate one, having a particular aim in mind. For instance, Jesus said, "For even the Son of Man did not come to be served, but to serve, and to give his life as a ransom for many" (Mark 10:45). He came to do something that He could not do where He was before arriving here. Possibly the best parallel for such use of the verb translated "to come" appears in the experiences of angels in the Old Testament. The angel Gabriel said to Daniel, "Daniel, I have now come to give you insight and understanding . . . I have come to tell you . . ." (Dan. 9:22, 23); " . . . your words were heard, and I have come in response to them" (Dan. 10:12).[3] The New Testament does not depict Christ as an angel, but "the advents of Christ and the angels are of the same kind" in that they both came from the heavenly realm with a particular purpose.[4] Again that presupposes His preexistence.

Divinity of Christ

With respect to Christ's incarnation, the Bible describes it as the incarnation of God. The Preexistent One was divine. During the night of Jesus' nativity the angels said to the shepherds, "Today in the town of David a Savior has been born to you; he is Christ the Lord" (Luke 2:11). The Jews were waiting for the coming of the Lord's Anointed, but the One who came was the Lord Himself. The Greek version of the Old Testament uses the term *kurios* ("Lord") to translate the Hebrew name Yahweh. In fact, throughout the New Testament we find Old Testament passages that originally described the work of the Lord/Yahweh being applied to Christ, thus indicating His divinity (e.g., Isa. 44:6/Rev. 1:17; Ps. 102:26, 27/Heb. 1:11, 12; Deut. 32:43/Heb. 1:6). Philippians 2:6-11 explicitly deals with the preexistence, divinity, incarnation, and exaltation of Christ. Before the Incarnation He was in His "very nature God" (verse 6), then during the Incarnation He "made himself nothing, taking the nature of a servant, being made in human likeness" (verse 7). As a human being "he humbled himself and became obedient to death—even death on a cross" (verse 8). Finally, through the resurrection He was exalted (verses 9-11). Here is a powerful narrative of the journey of the Son of God from the very presence of God to the chaos of our world.

John 8:56-58 brings the preexistence and divinity of the Son of God together. Jesus said to the Jewish leaders, "Your father Abraham rejoiced at the thought of seeing my day; he saw it and was glad" (verse 56). Understanding it to mean that Jesus had seen Abraham, they sarcastically wondered about it, since Jesus was not yet 50 years old! The answer was one they did not anticipate: "Before Abraham was born, I am!" (verse 58). Since the grammar of the sentence is not correct, we have to interpret the phrase "I am" as an allusion to the name of God in the Old Testament. In Exodus 3:14 the Lord revealed Himself to Moses as "I am who I am." Isaiah 43:10 contains the formula "I am he," and it then continues, "Before me no god was formed, nor will there be one after me. I, even I, am the Lord, and apart from me there is no savior" (verses 10, 11). Therefore, the "I am" designation affirms the supreme and exclusive superiority of God over any other deity. "Before Abraham was born, I am" is not simply a statement about "mere preexistence; it is eternal preexistence"[5]—the very existence of God.

A number of passages by New Testament writers explicitly refer to Jesus as God (e.g., Rom. 9:5; Heb. 1:8; Titus 2:13; 2 Peter 1:1). The most well known is

John 1:1: "In the beginning was the Word, and the Word was with God, and the Word was God." Again we find the preexistence and divinity of Jesus affirmed. The translation "the Word was God" is correct, as we see confirmed in John 1:18: "No one has ever seen God, but God the One and Only, who is at the Father's side, has made him known." God the Son reveals God the Father. Toward the end of the Gospel Thomas saw Jesus and exclaimed, "My Lord and my God!" (John 20:28). His response to the presence of the resurrected Lord was a Christian confession of faith.

Incarnation and Virgin Birth

John addresses the Incarnation when he writes: "The Word became flesh and made his dwelling among us" (John 1:14). The eternal Word of God, who was with God and who was also God, came to dwell among us. There is movement from the divine sphere to the human, described here as "flesh" (Greek, *sarx*). The revelation that Christ came in flesh was so important that John uses it to distinguish a true spirit from a false one (1 John 3:2), and true teachers from spurious ones (2 John 7). Paul echoes the same thought when he states that God sent "his own Son in the likeness of sinful man [*sarx*, "flesh"]" (Rom. 8:3).

In the Epistle to the Hebrews the incarnation of the Son of God plays a central role and is considered indispensable for His priestly ministry. He identified Himself with humans and "since the children have flesh and blood, he too shared in their humanity" (Heb. 2:14). The Son "had to be made like his brothers in every way" (verse 17), and it happened through the Incarnation. God prepared a body for Him (Heb. 10:5), and, in fact, "He appeared in a body" (1 Tim. 3:16). Consequently the apostle can talk about "the days of Jesus' life on earth" (Heb. 5:7) during which He suffered and was obedient to the will of God (Heb. 10:7). It is another way of expressing the same ideas found in Philippians 2:7—Christ "made himself nothing, taking the very nature of a servant, being made in human likeness." Galatians 4:4 presents the same mystery: "When the time had fully come, God sent his Son, born of a woman, born under law." Through the Incarnation He who "was rich . . . for your sakes . . . became poor" (2 Cor. 8:9). In the incarnated Savior "the fullness of the Deity lives in bodily form" (Col. 2:9).

When the angel said to Mary that she was to have a child, she asked him, "How will this be since I am a virgin?" (Luke 1:34). The angel answered, "The Holy Spirit will come upon you, and the power of the Most High will overshadow you. So the holy one to be born will be called the Son of God" (verse 35). Christian theology calls this the virginal conception of Jesus. Jesus was not the son of Joseph. Mary had already been pledged to be married to him, "but before they came together, she was found to be with child through the Holy Spirit" (Matt. 1:18). The angel informed Joseph that the child conceived in her was from the Holy Spirit (verse 20). In order to emphasize the virginal conception of Jesus, the biblical writer tells us that Joseph did not have a marital union with Mary "until she gave birth to a son" (verse 25). The promise God made to Eve in Genesis now had its fulfillment—the seed of the woman is the Savior. The virgin birth proclaims that salvation is from beginning to end the work of God and not of humans. Without it Jesus would have been a human being like any other human being, and not God in human flesh.

Humanity of Christ

Abundant biblical evidence also supports the claim that Jesus was a human being—that He had a human nature. Humans have been studying their own nature for centuries and have not been able to arrive at a universally accepted understanding of it. For our purpose I will suggest that according to the biblical creation narrative a human being is at least characterized by being a physical, an emotional, a spiritual, an intellectual, a social, and a moral entity. Jesus was a *physical being* whose body distinguished Him from other persons. He was born like any human being (Luke 2:7), and grew and became strong like any normal child (verse 40). People knew where He was born, who were His parents and brothers and sisters, and that He was a carpenter (Matt. 13:53-56). His body needed food (Matt. 4:2) and water (John 19:28) to preserve His life. Jesus got tired (John 4:6) and felt the need to sleep (Matt. 8:24). Finally He experienced death (Matt. 27:50). An *emotional being,* Jesus knew about the joy that comes through the power of the Spirit (Luke 10:21). But He also experienced sorrow (Matt. 26:38), could feel troubled (John 12:27; 13:21), and wept in the presence of friends (John 11:35) and during prayer (Heb. 5:7). Christ did not, however, have the negative emotions related to sin such as hatred toward others.

Jesus was a *spiritual being* who enjoyed having fellowship with the Father. Constantly He nurtured that fellowship with God through a life of prayer (Matt. 14:23; Mark 1:35) and through a life dedicated to the mission entrusted to Him (John 17:4). He had complete confidence in the guidance and presence of the Father in His life (John 11:41, 42). And He found in the observance of the Sabbath a magnificent opportunity to worship the Lord (Luke 4:16) and a day to teach and serve others (verse 31; 14:3, 4). As an *intellectual being* He grew in knowledge, was intelligent, and could reason with others—"filled with wisdom, and the grace of God was upon him" (Luke 2:40; cf. verse 52). When He was 12 years old, those who heard Him in the Temple were "amazed at his understanding and his answers" (verse 47; cf. Matt. 7:28, 29). A persuasive power in His speeches astounded His hearers.

Being a *social being,* Jesus constantly sought the company of others. He met with Jewish leaders and with sinners, prostitutes, non-Israelites, Roman officials, etc. Beyond that, He Himself longed for human companionship (Matt. 26:40, 43) and constantly had an interest in the needs of others (e.g., John 11:5). His life was indeed a public one open to anyone who wanted to approach Him. Above all, Jesus was the *moral being* par excellence. Having come to earth to do the will of the Father, He never deviated from that specific goal (e.g., John 8:28, 29). Even at the most crucial moment of His mission He submitted to the will of the Father and went to the cross (Matt. 26:42). It is particularly at this point that we find a fundamental discontinuity between Jesus and humans as we now know them. Morally and spiritually impeccable, He was sinless.

Sinless Jesus

Sin does not belong to the essence of being human. Therefore, the absence of sin in Christ does not question the fullness and legitimacy of His humanity. Because sin has damaged human nature by significantly corrupting its God-given original perfection, all now fall "short of the glory of God" (Rom. 3:23). To be genuinely human does not mean that one has to be a sinner. The witness of the New Testament is unanimous: Jesus was the Sinless One. Fully aware of that fact, He challenged His opponents to prove Him to be guilty of sin (John 8:46). He was conscious of the reality that He had always done the will of the Father (verse 29; 15:10), and that Satan "has no hold on me" (John 14:30), or "he has nothing in Me" (NASB).

During the Annunciation the angel referred to Jesus as "the holy one to be born" (Luke 1:35), and years later, after His ascension, Peter called Jesus "the Holy and Righteous One" (Acts 3:14; cf. 4:30; 13:35). The clear witness of Scripture is that "in him [Jesus] is no sin" (1 John 3:5), He "had no sin" (2 Cor. 5:21), He "was without sin" (Heb. 4:15), He was "a lamb without blemish or defect" (1 Peter 1:19), and "he committed no sin" (1 Peter 2:22). The fact that Jesus remained untouched by sin singles Him out as unique among human beings. It would be a mistake to equate His human nature with that of Adam, because He "took human nature, weakened and deteriorated by four thousand years of sin, yet undefiled and spotless."[6]

Nor should we interpret His sinlessness to mean that Jesus could not have sinned. After His baptism the enemy tempted Jesus in conditions that were far from ideal and yet He overcame him (Matt. 4:1-11). In Gethsemane He faced the temptation of not drinking the "cup," but He surrendered His will to that of the Father (Matt. 26:39). The possibility of falling into temptation or rebelling against the will of God does not necessarily presuppose a fallen human nature. All that it requires is freedom of the will. The cosmic conflict has indicated that free and perfect creatures, existing in the very presence of God, could choose to rebel against God. Freedom of the will can be misused, but Jesus chose never to abuse His. That He overcame every temptation and that He was free from sin were indispensable in His work of redemption and reconciliation. Atonement is firmly grounded in the sinlessness of Christ.

Union of the Two Natures

The union of the two natures in Christ continues to be an impenetrable mystery. Early in the history of the Christian church theologians debated the nature of that union and offered different and conflicting definitions of it.[7] In an effort to bring the debate to an end or to clarify it a church council convened in the city of Chalcedon in A.D. 451. The world has widely accepted the so-called Chalcedonian Definition. It established that Christ was truly God and truly human, that the property of each nature remained intact, and that the two natures were united in one person, the Son of God. Those same basic definitions also appear in the writings of Ellen G. White. According to her, the union was not that of two persons, but the union of the Son of God to human nature.[8] In it the divine nature "was not humanized; neither was humanity deified by the blending or union of the two natures; each retained its essential character and properties."[9] Humans "have reason, conscience, memory, will, affections."[10] Jesus "had reason, conscience, memory, will, and affections of the human soul which was united with His divine nature."[11] The Son of God indeed took human nature.

The fact that the two natures remained distinctive implies that it would be correct to suggest that in the Incarnation there existed two wills, the human and the divine. That helps us to understand the possibility that Jesus may have fallen into temptation.[12] God cannot be tempted to sin, but the human nature could. It also helps us to grasp that although the divine nature was omniscient, the human was not. The human nature grew in the understanding of the nature and mission of the Son of God (Luke 2:52).[13] That does not mean that the two natures were radically separated, and that therefore we have two persons instead of one. The divine and the human were united, and consequently, whatever the human nature experienced so did the divine nature. Here we should make careful distinctions. The divine nature experienced the feelings, emotions, struggles, and temptations of the human nature. For instance, when the human nature was thirsty, hungry, tempted, or anything else, the divine nature experienced in a unique and direct way what that experience meant for humans. It was the totality of the Person that experienced it. On the other hand, when the divine nature used divine power to heal, the human nature became the vehicle through which that power reached the other. When a sick woman touched Jesus' cloak and was healed, Mark says that "Jesus realized that power had gone out from him" (Mark 5:30). It was the power of the Son of God that healed the woman, but His human nature experienced in a unique way a divine power that it did not possess in itself. This was the result of the union of the two natures.[14] That union allowed the apostles to "apply qualities of both humanity and deity to the same person. Thus the One who upholds all things by the word of His power grew and became strong in stature and wisdom. He who was before Abraham was bon in a manger. The One who dies is the One who fills all in all."[15]

The Incarnation presupposes that in becoming human the eternal Son of God experienced limitations of some type. Interpreters have found it difficult to identify those limitations. In their discussion Philippians 2:6-11 has played a major role. As already indicated, the passage states that before the Incarnation Christ was God. It introduces the Incarnation with the phrase "[He] made himself nothing [kenoō, "to make empty"]" (Phil. 2:7). It would be inappropriate to argue that when He became human Christ emptied Himself of all or some of His divine attributes. In that case the Incarnation would not have been the full manifestation of God in human flesh. What, then, did Paul mean when he says that Christ "emptied Himself"?

I will suggest that the second part of Philippians 2:7 is an explanation of that phrase. He became nothing by "taking the very nature of a servant, being made in human likeness."[16] In other words, the self-emptying, the self-humiliation, of Christ consisted in becoming an obedient servant of God. The divine attributes and powers were limited in the sense that He would use them only as the Father saw fit and, therefore, in exclusive obedience to the Father.[17]

But we still have to ask, Did He not literally empty Himself of something? The answer has to be yes. Paul says: "For you know the grace of our Lord Jesus Christ, that though he was rich, yet for your sakes he became poor" (2 Cor. 8:9). It does not matter how we interpret "he was rich"; the fact that it is followed by "became poor" means that He emptied Himself of something when He became human. John seems to provide a glimmer of light into this mystery. Jesus prayed to the Father, "Glorify me in your presence with the glory I had with you before the world began" (John 17:5). The prayer presupposes that the Son "had enjoyed a unique glory with the Father in that preexistent state."[18] It may be right to conclude that "the sojourn of Jesus on earth does not then mean merely an irrelevant change in scene, but a forfeiture of that preworldly existence that he once possessed."[19]

We could argue that the verb translated as "made himself nothing" (Phil. 2:7) implies that the Son of God forfeited His original divine glory. If the verb kenoō refers to "divestiture of position or prestige,"[20] then we could say that when Christ clothed His divinity with humanity, "He was all the while as God, but He did not appear as God. He veiled the demonstrations of Deity which had commanded the homage, and called forth the admiration of the universe of God. He was God while upon earth, but divested Himself of the form of God, and in its stead took the form and fashion of a man. . . . He laid aside His glory and majesty. He was God, but the glories of the form of God He for a while relinquished."[21]

Conclusion

It is unquestionable that without the incarnation there would not be atonement. In the mystery of the incarnation God entered or invaded the sphere of His creatures in a unique way. He became permanently immanent among us and accessible to us in dimensions that we cannot fully comprehend. His sinless life made it possible for Him to die in the place of sinners. And His divinity, embodied in human flesh, paid for the penalty of sin and released grace and life for repentant sinners. In coming down, He revealed not only God's sacrificial love but also the Lord's ideal for human beings. Christ provided an example for us to follow as we through the power of the Spirit become more and more like Him.

---

[1] Paul J. Achtemeier, *1 Peter: A Commentary on First Peter* (Minneapolis: Fortress, 1996), pp. 131, 132.

[2] For a thorough discussion of that formula see Simon J. Gathercole, *The Preexistent Son: Recovering the Christology of Matthew, Mark, and Luke* (Grand Rapids: Eerdmans, 2006), pp. 83-176.

[3] *Ibid.*, pp. 119-121.

[4] *Ibid.*, p. 147.

[5] Raoul Dederen, "Christ: His Person and Work," in *Handbook of Seventh-day Adventist Theology*, ed. Raoul Dederen (Hagerstown, Md.: Review and Herald, 2000), p. 162.

[6] *Ibid.*, p. 165.

[7] For a summary of the discussions, see Wayne Grudem, *Systematic Theology: An Introduction to Biblical Doctrine* (Grand Rapids: Zondervan, 1994), pp. 554-558.

[8] Ellen G. White commented: "The two natures were mysteriously blended in one person— the man Christ Jesus" (*Lift Him Up* [Hagerstown, Md.: Review and Herald, 1988], p. 76).

[9] Ellen G. White, *Manuscript Releases* (Silver Spring, Md.: E. G. White Estate, 1993), vol. 16, p. 182.

[10] Ellen G. White, *Selected Messages* (Washington, D.C.: Review and Herald, 1980), book 3, p. 130.

[11] Ellen G. White, *Manuscript Releases*, vol. 16, p. 182.

[12] "The divine nature, combined with the human, made Him capable of yielding to Satan's temptations" (*ibid.*). We have no need to speculate concerning what would have happened had the human will yielded to the temptation, because it did not!

[13] "While Christ was teaching others, He Himself was receiving light and knowledge about His own work and mission in the world; for it is plainly stated that Christ 'grew in knowledge'" (Ellen G. White, in *Youth's Instructor*, Nov. 28, 1895). "As Jesus looked upon the offerings that were brought as a sacrifice to the Temple, the Holy Spirit taught Him that His life was to be sacrificed for the life of the world" (Ellen G. White, in *Youth's Instructor*, Dec. 12, 1895).

[14] The miracles of Jesus were the result of His divine power. Ellen G. White states: "Jesus revealed His divinity by His mighty miracles" (*The Desire of Ages*, p. 608). They provided "unmistakable evidence of the divinity" of Christ (*The Spirit of Prophecy* [Battle Creek, Mich.: Steam Press, 1878], vol. 3, p. 145). He never used His divine power for His personal benefit: "He who worked miracles for others worked none for Himself. He had clothed His divinity with humanity, and He had come to bring divine power to man. He met the enemy at every step with 'It is written'" (Ellen G. White, in *Signs of the Times*, Sept. 30, 1889).

[15] Dederen, p. 169.

[16] See Gordon D. Fee, "The New Testament and Kenosis Christology," in *Exploring Kenotic Christology: The Self-Emptying of God*, ed. C. Stephen Evans (Oxford: University Press, 2006),

pp. 32, 33.

[17] One could perhaps say that "it seems probable that when he healed the sick, revealed what was in people, and raised the dead, he considered those appropriate occasions for revealing more of his divine capabilities. Each of these revelations of his divine nature was carried out in harmony with the leading of the Holy Spirit and in fulfillment of the Father's purposes" (Gordon R. Lewis and Bruce A. Demarest, *Integrative Theology* [Grand Rapids: Zondervan, 1994], p. 285).

[18] Leon Morris, *Commentary on the Gospel of John* (Grand Rapids: Eerdmans, 1971), p. 721.

[19] Ernst Haenchen, *John 2: A Commentary of the Gospel of John 7-21* (Philadelphia: Fortress, 1984), p. 152.

[20] F. W. Danker, *Greek-English Lexicon*, p. 539.

[21] *The Seventh-day Adventist Bible Commentary*, Ellen G. White Comments, vol. 7-A, p. 446. In another place she comments: "He who was the Commander in the heavenly courts laid aside His royal robe and kingly crown, and clothing His divinity with humanity, came to this world to stand at the head of the human race" (*ibid.*, vol. 7, p. 904).

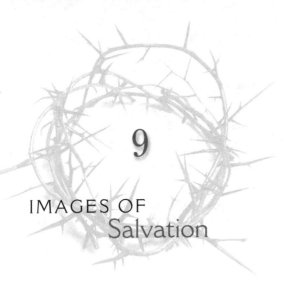

9

IMAGES OF
Salvation

The sacrificial death of Christ on the cross is like a diamond. In order to appreciate its beauty, we must examine it from different angles and allow it to reflect light from different facets. Each angle reveals particular details that we could have otherwise easily missed. The significance of the death of Christ cannot be totally captured in one specific expression of it. The diversity of images used enriches our comprehension. In the biblical text the various images intersect each other, making it difficult to discuss one in isolation. The common element in all of them appears to be the sacrificial understanding of Christ's death. We will discuss only a few of those images.

Redemption

The New Testament interprets Jesus' death as an act of redemption. The concept of redemption weaves throughout Scripture from Matthew (Matt. 20:28) to Revelation (Rev. 5:9). It was a concept widely used in the marketplace during the New Testament period. The terminology designated the redemption of prisoners of war and slaves through a ransom. The usage of the concept in the New Testament is influenced primarily by the meaning of redemption in the Old Testament.

Old Testament background. In Israel it was possible to redeem persons, animals, and properties. Those cases that directly associate God with redemption interest us particularly. The legislation dealing with the redemption of the firstborn of animals and humans is also useful. Such legislation was based on the fact that during the tenth plague of Egypt, God preserved the life of all the firstborn of the Israelites. Israelites were to sacrifice the firstborn of clean animals to Him, but in the case of unclean animals redemption was necessary. For instance, the firstborn of a donkey, an unclean animal, could be redeemed by giving to the Lord a lamb. If it was not redeemed, they were to kill it by breaking its neck (Ex. 13:13). In this case redemption consisted in legally releasing what belonged to the Lord (the firstborn of an ass) through a substitute (a lamb) in order for it to be useful to the new owner. It was not an act of buying back, because the donkey originally belonged to the Lord. The Israelites could keep the unclean animal through a redemptive substitute or through the payment of a ransom (Num. 18:14-16). The firstborn of humans also had to be redeemed, because God did not accept human sacrifices. The redemption occurred through the payment of a specific amount of money, the redemption price (Num. 18:15, 16; cf. Ex. 13:13, 15). The Lord accepted the money in place of the life of the firstborn. Such legal contexts associate the concept of redemption with substitution, a redemption payment (a ransom), and with deliverance.

In the Old Testament God is the ultimate Redeemer. He has become the closest relative of Israel and acts on its behalf to redeem it from oppressors. The Lord brought Israel into existence by redeeming it from Egypt (Ex. 6:6; 15:13; Deut. 9:26; Ps. 106:10). Here the idea of deliverance predominates without any reference to payment. The same applies to many cases in which God redeems individuals from a multiplicity of difficulties and life-threatening situations (e.g., Ps. 31:4, 5; 26:11; Jer. 15:21), and to the future eschatological redemption (Isa. 1:27, 28; Micah 4:10; Hosea 7:13; 13:14; Jer. 50:34). Throughout the Old Testament redemption designates fundamentally deliverance, a change of ownership, often as a result of a redemption payment.

The concept of redemption reaches new heights of meaning when put into the context of human sin. In that case Scripture exhorts Israel to put its hope in the Lord, knowing that with Him there "is full redemption," that is to say, that "He himself will redeem Israel from all their sins" (Ps. 130:7, 8). The psalmist does not tell us how the Lord will accomplish that all-encompassing redemption. It is only through the sacrificial system that we gain some insights on the topic. We have already indicated that the life of the repentant sinner was preserved at the cost of the life of the sacrificial victim (Lev. 17:11; Heb. *kofer*, "ransom"). The life of the sacrifice functioned as a ransom-substitute for the person. The Old Testament acknowledges that the redemption of human life lies beyond what humans could accomplish. The psalmist confesses that "no man can redeem the life of another or give to God a ransom for him—the ransom for a life is costly, no payment is ever enough—that he should live on forever and not see decay" (Ps. 49:7-9). Only the Lord can accomplish such a redemption: "God will redeem my life from the grave; he will surely take me to himself" (verse 15). We are close to the ideas found in Isaiah 53.

Redemption in the New Testament. In the New Testament redemption designates the end result and/or the process of redemption. When it stresses the end result, it does not explicitly state the idea of a ransom/a payment. In such cases, the consequence of redemption is deliverance or salvation (Luke 1:68; 2:38; 24:21). It is also the case when the New Testament describes redemption as an eschatological expectation, such as the future "redemption of our bodies" (Rom. 8:23); "the day of redemption" (Eph. 4:30; cf. Luke 21:28; Eph. 1:4). In such contexts redemption is a synonym for salvation. We would like to pay particular attention to those passages that address or hint at the how of redemption. Most such cases use sacrificial terminology and ideology.

The first text that we will examine is Ephesians 1:7: "In him we have redemption through his blood, the forgiveness of sins, in accordance with the riches of God's grace." The context of the text discusses God's "glorious grace" that we have received "freely" in Christ. That grace manifested itself in an act of redemption. The mention of "blood" introduces a sacrificial understanding of Christ's death. Redemption is accomplished here through Christ's sacrificial death. The passage further defines redemption as "forgiveness of sins" and brings atonement and forgiveness together here in the same fashion as in Leviticus 4. In Leviticus the sacrificial victim was offered as an atoning sacrifice and then the sin of the people or the individual was forgiven by the Lord (Lev. 4:20, 26, 30). Redemption was deliverance from sin. Now it is accomplished not through the blood of animals given as a ransom, but through the blood of Christ. What the believer received freely was very costly to God.

The second passage we will examine is 1 Peter 1:18, 19: "For you know that it was not with perishable things such as silver or gold that you were redeemed from the empty way of life . . . , but with the precious blood of Christ, a lamb without blemish or defect." The text contains several important ideas. First, the introductory clause—"for you know"—implies that Peter refers to something already familiar to his readers because it was part of the common Christian teachings. It was part of the traditional Christian interpretation of Christ's death. Second, redemption takes place here through the payment of a ransom, a conclusion supported by the context. Peter introduces the payment with a negative clause: the price paid was not gold or silver. He rejects the value of such payment for our redemption, because gold and silver are corruptible—they are perishable. Then follows a contrastive, positive statement: The real price was the "precious [timios] blood of Christ." The word timios means not just "precious" but also "costly." The price paid to redeem believers was a high one. Here we find the answer to the concern of the psalmist in Psalm 49:8, 9.

Third, according to Peter redemption occurs through the sacrificial death of Christ. He makes it clear that in the apostolic understanding of the atonement believers interpreted the expression "blood of Christ" in sacrificial terms. He explicitly states that Christ's sacrificial blood was that of a sacrificial lamb without blemish or defect. The reference is not just to the Passover lamb but to sacrificial victims in general (cf. Ex. 29:30; Lev. 12:6), and probably to Isaiah 53:7 (cf. 1 Peter 2:21, 22).[1] Believers were redeemed from their "empty way of life" handed down to them from their forefathers. This refers to their former sinful way of life characterized by darkness (1 Peter 2:9). Christ bore their sins in order for them to be free from the power of sin (1 Peter 2:24; 3:18). The contrast between the blood/life of Christ and gold and silver suggests that in order to redeem humanity, life was given in place of the life of sinners. This understanding of Christ's death goes back to Jesus himself.

The third text is Mark 10:45: "For even the Son of Man did not come to be served, but to serve, and to give his life as a ransom for many." The text possibly alludes to Isaiah 53. First, we find three linguistic connections between it and Isaiah 53:11, 12: "to give," "his life," and "many." It is enough to argue for the dependence of the one on the other. Second, we also notice a conceptual connection. Both passages have the idea of substitution. The Servant suffers and dies vicariously, and so does the Son of man. In this case the preposition "for" (*'anti*) is very important. Meaning "in place of, instead of," it clearly expresses the idea of substitution. One could argue that we could translate *'anti* as "to the advantage of," but the text is stating that had it not been for Jesus and what happened to Him, the many would have also suffered. Therefore, He took their place.[2]

Implicit in the text is the idea that the life of the many was in jeopardy. Unless something special took place the "many" would have perished. Christ came to pay the price for their liberation from death. He surrendered His own life as a substitutive ransom for them. This fits very well with that Jesus said in Mark 8:37. In the context of the announcement of His own death, He raised the rhetorical question "What can a man give in exchange for his soul?" The obvious answer was a negative one. But our passage, Mark 10:45, provides the ultimate answer. Paul expressed the same idea, saying that Christ gave "himself as a ransom [*'anti-lutron*] for [*hupér*] all men" (1 Tim. 2:6). In this particular case, the preposition *'anti* was prefixed to the noun *lútron* ("ransom"), which is followed by the preposition *hupér* ("for, on behalf of"). Both the preposition and the prefix serve to emphasize the idea of substitution. Christ's life was a ransom given not just for our benefit but particularly in our place.

The fourth passage is Galatians 3:13, in which the apostle states that "Christ redeemed [*'exagorazō*] us from the curse of the law by becoming a curse for us." The verb *'exagorazō* means "to redeem, to purchase," and appears in Greek legal contexts to indicate the manumission of slaves. The book of Galatians employs the verb to refer to redemption from the curse of the law. Here is an important passage that deserves some careful attention. First, the curse of the law falls upon those who, while trying to keep the whole law, demonstrate in their own experience the human incapacity truly to fulfill it (verse 10). The result of the curse is death. For Paul, "the whole world is a prisoner of sin" (verse 22), and he identifies the law as the gatekeeper to the prison—all are "under the law" (verse 23, KJV). Since the law cannot give life (verse 21), and humans are unable by themselves to fulfill its demands, they find themselves under the curse of the law—that is to say, condemned by it.

Second, Paul upholds the claim of the law—its curse. God ordains that curse, and it expresses His will toward unrepentant sinners. The apostle does not question its validity, but rather reaffirms it. The curse of the law occupies a legal place in human experience as a consequence of rebellion. The universality of sin means that the condemnatory function of the law touches everyone. Third, the claim of the law must be satisfied. Nothing can cancel, neutralize, or ignore it. The judgment of the law against sinners must be accomplished because it is a right judgment. Surprisingly, Paul announces that the righteous claim of the law, its curse against sinners, was fully satisfied in the death of Christ. It was actualized on the innocent One. By taking what was ours, He went through what we should otherwise have had to experience. This is redemptive substitution.

Fourth, through Christ's vicarious death we find ourselves redeemed from the curse of the law. He became a curse "for us" (*huper*). The fact that the concept of substitution is present in the context supports the suggestion that the preposition *huper* expresses the idea of substitution. Christ's act of redemption was sacrificial because in the process He died. It is also vicarious because He accepted the mortal curse of the law for us/in our place.

Galatians 3:13 clearly indicates that humans were alienated from God and under the curse of the law. The curse does not act independently of God, but it is rather an expression of the divine will and, therefore, reveals His righteous attitude toward sin and sinners. Deliverance from that state of condemnation occurs only through the redemptive and substitutive death of Christ. In this redemptive act "justice is not thrust aside, but justice is satisfied."[3]

New Testament writers interpret Christ's death as an act of redemption. A price was paid for the salvation of fallen human beings.[4] In order to express the costliness of redemption, the New Testament found it necessary to combine it with the sacrificial understanding of Christ's death. The biblical authors realized that the price was extremely high, namely, the life of Christ. Life was given in place of life. The cursed ones were redeemed by Him who became the cursed one. The New Testament does not ask: To whom was the ransom given? If someone is to be identified, it would be God.

Reconciliation

The interpretation of the death of Christ as an act of reconciliation comes from social interaction. Commentators have generally considered it to refer to the restoration of good and proper relationships between former enemies. The process of restoring harmony usually demands a mediator. In the New Testament reconciliation is not simply the experience of individuals. God seeks to restore harmony to the totality of the cosmos through the work of Christ (Col. 1:20). For now, we will pay close attention to 2 Corinthians 5:18-21, one of the most important passages on the topic of reconciliation in the New Testament. We will first examine its structure.[5]

18. All this is from God,
    A   who reconciled us to himself through Christ
    B   and gave us the ministry of reconciliation
19. That is,
    A'   God was reconciling the world to himself in Christ,
        not counting men's sins against them.
    B'   And he has committed to us the message of reconciliation.

20. B   We are therefore Christ's ambassadors,
       as though God were making his appeal through us.
       We implore you on Christ's behalf: Be reconciled to God.
21 A   God made him who had no sin to be sin for us,
       so that in him we might become the righteousness of God.

Reconciliation and believers. The text makes several closely related statements about the divine act of reconciliation. The ideas develop and repeat themselves throughout the verses—notice the A B A' B' parallel structure. The parallelism is basically developmental and serves to explain what Paul meant by reconciliation and how it took place. In the first statement he describes the situation of the Christian community: God, through Christ, "reconciled us to himself and gave us the ministry of reconciliation." These two ideas will further enlarge. For now, notice that the verbs are in the past tense—"reconciled" and "gave." God did for believers two things—namely, reconciled them, and gave them the ministry of reconciliation. The past tenses indicate that for Christians reconciliation is a fully accomplished fact.

God the Reconciler. Verse 19 broadens the reconciliation beyond the horizon of believers, reinforcing at the same time the idea that in the work of reconciliation God took the initiative: "God was reconciling the world to himself in Christ." Had it not been for God taking the lead, humans would have remained alienated from Him forever. They could do absolutely nothing to restore a harmonious relationship between them and God. The fact that God took the first step when they were sinners reveals His loving character. He not only had the desire to reconcile humans to Him; He also provided the means to accomplish it.

Paul introduces the method of reconciliation by the use of the prepositions "through" (*dia*; verse 18) and "in/through" (*en*; verse 19) Christ. It clearly suggests that reconciliation presupposes divine love. The Mediator of reconciliation did not have to change God's attitude toward us from hostility to love. The text does not state that God was reconciling Himself to us, as if He had offended us. Rather, He was reconciling us to Himself because we were the alienated and rebellious party. He is always the subject of the verb and never the object of reconciliation. As we will show, this does not mean that God was indifferent to human sin and rebellion.

Nature of reconciliation. What we have just stated raises the question of the nature of the reconciliation that the apostle speaks about. As we have already indicated, commentators usually interpret reconciliation to mean that a peaceful relationship has been reestablished between former enemies. But if God was reconciling the world *in Christ*, then the individual (the sinner) was not personally affected by it—he or she was not really reconciled. Then in what sense can we speak here about the reconciliation of the world? This is what the rest of the passage clarifies for us. Verse 19 introduces new information not found in verse 18. It mentions two further actions by God that explain how He brought about reconciliation and what it entails. The first divine action was "not counting men's sins against them." What made it impossible for humans to have fellowship with God was not His attitude toward us, which as we have already stressed was always a loving one, but sin—our own sin—which required an expression of God's wrath.

Therefore, from God's perspective reconciliation means removing that which made it impossible for us to have fellowship with Him—sin. We can then suggest that reconciliation took place in God's loving heart at the moment He determined not to count human sin against them. "God was reconciling the world to himself" would then mean that He unilaterally decided to put away His own condemnation and wrath against a sinful world in order to reconcile them with Himself. How could that be possible? He placed their sin on Christ, who thus assumed responsibility for it—a concept expressed in verse 21. That verse develops the meaning of the phrase "not counting men's sins against them." That is to say, God did not give to the human race what they deserved on account of their sin. Instead, He actually placed that sin—the sins of rebellious humanity and the proper penalty for them—on Christ.

As a result it is extremely difficult to avoid the conclusion that Paul is dealing here with the ideas of transfer of sin and substitution. It was only because Christ was without sin that He was able to bear the sins of others. In other words, the sin that was not counted against the world was counted against Christ. We detect here an echo of Isaiah 53:6, 10, and 12. God is not morally indifferent to

106

sin. But Christ experienced the necessary penalty for it: "For Christ's love compels us, because we are convinced that one died for all, and therefore all died" (2 Cor. 5:14). The preposition "for" carries with it the idea of substitution. The provision of reconciliation is so abundant that there is no reason for anyone to die, to be eternally lost. Christ experienced the alienation of all as their substitute and exhausted it in His self-sacrifice.

Since there was now no obstacle for full fellowship with God, God then initiated His second act in the work of reconciliation. He brought into existence the "ministry of reconciliation," which consists of the proclamation of the "message of reconciliation." But it is not a human work or task. Paul says that "we are Christ's ambassadors," but that it is God who is "making his appeal through us." When we as Christians tell the world, "Be reconciled to God," we are doing it on behalf of Christ.

The clear implication of this analysis is that "the total act of reconciliation on God's side is in two parts. There is the act of reconciliation in Christ, and there is the ministry of reconciliation which consists in the proclamation of this prior act of God in Christ" as an appeal to humans to be reconciled to God.[6] The divine act of reconciliation is not completed until humans respond to the offer of reconciliation. In other words, "the message proclaimed by the apostle is *part* of the reconciling activity which God has been doing in Christ; it is not just a device constructed so that men can appropriate what God has done in Christ."[7]

Therefore, the divine act of reconciliation includes the work of God in Christ on the cross that consisted in the removal of the barrier of sin—i.e., not counting it against us—and the creation and implementation of the ministry of reconciliation. One could perhaps talk about three acts in the reconciliation of the world. The first two are objective realities, the exclusive work of God, namely, His removing our sin by placing it on Christ, and creating the ministry of reconciliation. The third one is a subjective experience that happens when humans listen to what God did for them on the cross and let the Spirit move them to put an end to their hostility against God.

Finally, Paul does not say that "God *reconciled* the world to Himself." The verbal form he uses—"was reconciling"—indicates that reconciliation is a process rather than something that took place at one specific point in time. This is required by Paul's understanding of reconciliation as consisting of three stages and not as just one that occurred in the past. It is interesting to notice that the verb of "*not counting* men's sins against them" is a present participle, suggesting that the action it describes "is considered timeless and therefore present."[8] It is something that God is still doing. On the other hand, God "gave" the ministry of reconciliation to the church—a past action. It is only the totality of the divine activity that we can properly call reconciliation.

At this point it will be useful to go back to 2 Corinthians 5:21: "God made him [Christ] who had no sin to be sin for us, so that in him we might become the righteousness of God." The purpose of God's act of reconciliation was to justify us by faith. Once we are justified by faith the objective act of reconciliation reaches its fullness: "Therefore, since we have been justified through faith, we have peace with God through our Lord Jesus Christ" (Rom. 5:1). Reconciliation and justification are not the same, but have a close association.

Justification

The New Testament takes the image of justification from the court of law and uses it to interpret the significance of Christ's death. Romans 5:10, 11 and 2 Corinthians 5:18-21 bring together reconciliation and justification by faith. They are almost synonymous. Yet they still express different ideas. What allows us to bring them together is the fact that both are divine actions made possible through the sacrificial death of Christ. According to Romans 5:9, "We have . . . been justified by his blood." Justification is a reality only because Christ died as a sacrificial victim for us.

In any interpretation of the sacrificial death of Christ and its relationship with justification by faith, Romans 3:21-26 must play a significant role. First, Paul had been arguing that Gentiles and Jews were under the judgment of God—accountable to Him (verse 19). The word translated "to be accountable" (*hupodikos*) means "answerable to." The apostle depicts humanity as standing before the divine tribunal, proven guilty and awaiting God's condemnation. Second, God provided what humans needed, namely, a means of justification. The Lord displayed Christ, or "presented him as a sacrifice of atonement, through faith in his blood" (verse 25). Since humans could not atone for their own sin in order to be accepted by Him, God provided the sacrificial victim they needed. We find here a fulfillment of Leviticus 17:11, in which the Lord Himself provided for the Israelites the means of atonement through the blood of the sacrificial victim on the altar.

Third, Paul announces the good news that "now" God, through Christ's death, is declaring believers innocent, righteous before Him (Rom. 3:21). The Christ event reveals this righteousness, and it is available to those who place their faith in Him. It is a free gift of divine grace. How could God justify those who believe? Through Christ's *redemptive* work. Redemption was possible because God presented Christ as an expiatory sacrifice. The phrase "by his blood" most probably indicates the price of redemption and could be translated "at the price/cost of his blood." His redemptive sacrifice provided the ground for God's acquittal of repentant sinners. It was necessary because humanity was facing God's judgment and wrath. Fourth, the justification that is by faith is grounded in the sacrificial death of Christ as our substitute. The death sentence pronounced against humans in the divine tribunal was executed not on them but on Christ, who died in their place. Out of that atoning event God willingly declares repentant sinners innocent, acquitted of all charges. Paul makes clear that Christ's death liberates humanity from sin and its penalty.

Fifth, by dealing with sin in the person of a sacrificial substitute, God showed that He did not take it lightly. Even in grace He did not compromise His justice. The cross revealed both God's true attitude toward sin and that He is righteous in the way He has both dealt with and is now dealing with it. On the one hand, God revealed His justice in condemning the sinners; on the other hand, He displayed His mercy in redeeming and justifying them. The cross indeed demonstrates His saving and punitive justice. The death of Jesus beautifully combined mercy and justice.

Finally, Christ's expiatory sacrifice enriches the meaning of justification and redemption. Paul establishes a close connection between sacrifice, justification, and redemption. The basic concept is that of sacrifice. Without His sacrifice, redemption and justification were impossible. Romans 3:21-26 relates justification to cultic terminology. The Old Testament does not limit the vocabulary of justification to the legal sphere. This terminology is also important in the cult—the rituals of the sacrificial system. The declaration of justice was pronounced also in the Temple (Ps. 24:3-6; 15:1, 2). Legal and cultic concepts as well as forensic and redemptive convictions found common ground in the sacrificial system.

Expiatory/Propitiatory Sacrifice

We have already indicated that the Bible uses the image of a substitutive sacrifice to interpret the meaning of Christ's death. At this point, we would like to discuss the objective of that sacrifice. Is it an expiatory or a propitiatory sacrifice? That is to say, does it aim at accomplishing something for humans (expiation) or at changing God's attitude toward humans (propitiation)? While expiation refers to the removal of the obstacle for fellowship with God, propitiation expresses the idea of appeasing God, presupposing the presence of divine wrath toward the sinner. The terminology used in the New Testament to express the idea of expiation could also communicate the concept of propitiation. We could translate the verb *hilaskomai* in Hebrews 2:17 as either to "propitiate" or to "expiate," but in this case "expiation" is the better rendering. Its derivatives *hilasmos* ("propitiation, expiation"—1 John 2:2; 4:10) and *hilasterion* ("instrument of expiation, propitiation"—Rom. 3:25) convey the same ideas.[9] One should acknowledge that the primary perspective in those texts appears to be that of expiation. However, the idea of propitiation is not totally absent, particularly the case in Romans 3:25. The context of that passage is precisely a discussion of God's wrath against sinners (Rom. 1:18; 2:2, 4, 5, 8, 16; 3:4-6).[10] Within that framework Paul describes Christ as the person who freed us from that wrath. The usage in 1 John and the wider context of the epistle also points to the idea of propitiation by identifying Christ as our mediator before God. According to John, death is the result of God's judgment (1 John 2:28; 4:17, 18) and unbelief (1 John 2:17; 3:14).[11] Only the sacrifice of Christ brings freedom from death.

Divine wrath against sin is real. But here we should be careful not to give the impression that the Son had to persuade the Father to love us by becoming the object of His unloving and vengeful wrath. The word "propitiation," if we choose to employ it, we should understand or define biblically as divine self-propitiation—that is to say, God in Christ propitiated Himself, was moved by His own love. It was out of that love that God sent His Son as an expiation/propitiation for our sins (1 John 4:10). We must emphasize that "this is not the pagan idea that an angry god may be appeased by sacrifice: for God himself provides the means of propitiation and justification. In Christ, God himself absorbs the destructive consequences of sin. Hence the gospel creates a division between those who are freed from wrath through trust in God's merciful love (1 Thess. 1:10; 5:9; Rom. 5:9) and those who remain under wrath because they despise his mercy (Rom. 2:4-5, 8; 9:22-23; Eph. 2:3; 5:6; Col. 3:6)."[12]

Theater of God's Love

The New Testament portrays the death of Christ as a revelation of God's love for sinners. John explicitly says that God showed/made known His love for us by sending His Son to give us life (1 John 4:9). It is "not that we loved God, but that he loved us and sent his Son as an atoning sacrifice for our sins" (verse 10). Paul adds: "But God demonstrates his own love for us in this: While we were still sinners, Christ died for us" (Rom. 5:8; cf. Eph. 2:4, 5). The manifestation of His divine love took place on the cross before we could personally and fully benefit from it—even before we were willing to accept it. In the revelation of that love God did not first base His action on whether we would accept it or not, but simply took the initiative and sent His Son to reveal the inscrutable depth of His love for us (John 3:16).

Jesus clarified, "But I, when I am lifted up from the earth, will draw [helko] all men to myself" (John 12:32). The verb helko means "to draw, drag," but in the case of persons it means "to compel, to draw." In the Gospel of John it seems to describe God's beneficent wooing for salvation. Jesus said, "No one can come to me unless the Father who sent me draws [helko] him" (John 6:44). Humans are unable to come to God, and consequently the Father displayed His love for us on the cross in order to pull us to Him. It is this sublime manifestation of divine love that will bring the cosmic conflict to an end.

In Christian theology a whole theory of the atonement developed that focused exclusively on the model of the cross as a revelation of God's love. Called the moral influence theory of the atonement, it argues that the atoning power of the death of Christ is located only within the effect it has on sinners. It understands the cross as a revelation of the character of God as a loving being, and it is that revelation that transforms sinners. For theologians that support this interpretation "the predicament from which man requires to be delivered is not that of bondage to sin or demonic powers, but *ignorance or misunderstanding concerning God.*"[13] Those who promote the theory reject the biblical teaching of the substitutionary death of Jesus on the cross.

Many often argue that it is legally incorrect for an innocent person to die in place of the guilty, particularly if God is the one inflicting the punishment on the innocent. We agree that if a judge were to make the innocent suffer and die in order to deliver the guilty we would be witnessing a violation of the integrity of a legal system. But such reasoning implies that there are three persons involved in the process: the guilty party, an innocent person, and a judge. The judge then orders or allows the innocent party to receive the punishment deserved by the guilty one, setting the guilty individual free. That is not the case in the atonement. The atonement is what God Himself, and only God, has done for us. It is a matter between God and us. No third party is involved! The Innocent One who dies in place of the sinner is no one else than God in human flesh. He also is the one against whom we sinned. Jesus was consubstantial with the Father and as the representative of the Godhead He offered Himself willingly to assume responsibility for our sin.[14] Henceforth, substitutionary atonement is indeed the greatest revelation of the love of God. It is blasphemous to accuse Him of being immoral when in fact He decided to assume responsibility for our sin in order to show His loving grace to undeserving sinners. Who would dare to consider God unjust because He forgives those who offended Him by taking upon Himself their load of sin?

Any attempt to define the meaning of the cross exclusively in terms of a revelation of love, i.e., without taking into consideration sacrificial substitution, is not only one-sided but also unfaithful to the saving message of the Bible. Christ's death "must benefit us if it is to reveal love for us. It will not do to say that it benefits us because, or in the sense that, it reveals love. That would be to argue in circle."[15] Thus Christ's death is indeed the greatest revelation of divine love *because* in it "God was reconciling the world to Himself . . . , not counting men's sins against them," but rather making "him who had no sin to be sin for us" (2 Cor. 5:19, 21).

Conclusion

The apostolic church proclaimed the redemptive work of a crucified Savior—a particularly shameful way of dying. The question that early Christians faced was one of the meaning of that particular crucifixion. The Old Testament background helped, guided by the teachings of Jesus and the presence of the Spirit, to unpack the meaning of the hideous death of Christ. The typological significance of the sacrificial system provided a foundational theological frame of reference. The church interpreted the humiliating death of Jesus as a substitutionary, expiatory, and propitiatory sacrifice through which God redeemed, reconciled, and justified us, revealing the unfathomable depths of His sacrificial love. But the question still remains: How did Christ's sacrificial death accomplish all the above? What really happened on the cross?

---

[1] J. Ramsey Michaels, *1 Peter* (Waco, Tex.: Word, 1988), p. 66.

[2] F. Büchsel, "*Lútron*," in *Theological Dictionary of the New Testament*, vol. 4, p. 343.

[3] Herman Ridderbos, *Paul: An Outline of His Theology* (Grand Rapids: Eerdmans, 1975), p. 196.

[4] Redemption is also illustrated through the use of the image of the marketplace. The New Testament occasionally uses the verb *agorazō* ("to buy") to refer to the work of Christ on behalf of believers. They belong to God because they "were bought with a price" (1 Cor. 6:19, 20, KJV; 7:23, KJV; cf. 2 Peter 2:1). The price paid is mentioned in Revelation 5:9: "You are worthy to take the scroll and to open its seals, because you were slain [*sphazō*], and with your blood you purchased men for God." Here it describes Christ's death as a sacrificial one. He was the "Lamb" (verse 6) whose blood was used to pay for the redemption of humanity. Revelation 5:9 indicates the price through the phrase *en tō haimati* ("with the blood"). The preposition *'en* stands here for the genitive of price and should be translated "at the price of [His blood]."

[5] This structure is taken from Howard Marshall ("Meaning of Reconciliation," in *Unity and Diversity in New Testament Theology*, ed. Robert A. Guelich [Grand Rapids: Eerdmans, 1978], p. 122), with modifications suggested by Stanley E. Porter (*Katallassō in Ancient Greek Literature With Reference to the Pauline Writings* [Cordoba, Spain: Ediciones el Almendro, 1994], p. 128).

[6] Marshall, p. 122.

[7] Richard T. Mead, "Exegesis of 2 Corinthians 5:14-21," in *Interpreting 2 Corinthians 5:14-21: An Exercise in Hermeneutics*, ed. Jack P. Lewis [Lewiston, N.Y.: Edwin Mellen Press, 1989], pp. 155, 156.

[8] *Ibid.*, p. 155.

[9] The predominant meaning of that word family in Greek literature is that of propitiation; see Jintae Kim, "The Concept of Atonement in Hellenistic Thought and in 1 John," *Journal of Greco-Roman Christianity and Judaism* 2 (2001-2005): 100-116.

[10] See Raoul Dederen, "Christ," pp. 178-180.

[11] With M. A. Seifrid, "Death of Christ," in *Dictionary of the Later New Testament and Its Developments*, eds. Ralph P. Martin and Peter H. Davids (Downers Grover, Ill.: InterVarsity, 1997), p. 282. Also, Georg Strecker, *The Johannine Letters* (Minneapolis: Fortress, 1996), p. 39, in which he writes, "The concrete idea of Jesus' 'propitiatory sacrifice' should not be excluded; it accords with the preceding argumentation (1 John1:7: *haima Iesou* [blood of Jesus]; 1:9: *katharisē hēmas* [he cleansed us])."

[12] S. M. Travis, "Wrath of God (New Testament)," in *Anchor Bible Dictionary*, vol. 6, p. 997.

[13] Alister McGrath, "The Moral Theory of the Atonement: An Historical and Theological Critique," *Scottish Journal of Theology* 38 (1985): 211.

[14] See Robert Letham, *The Work of Christ* (Downers Grove, Ill.: InterVarsity, 1993), p. 137.

[15] John Knox, *The Death of Christ: The Cross in New Testament History and Faith* (New York: Abingdon Press, 1958), p. 151.

10

THE MEANING OF THE CROSS:
Atonement as Divine *Pathema*/Suffering

Jesus was heading to Jerusalem for the last time. It was the defining moment in His mission to our planet and the reason for His heavenly descent. After this visit nothing would remain the same. About to experience the unimaginable in the hands of humans and in the realm of darkness, He journeyed under the shadow of the cross, anticipating it. The cosmic conflict was going to find in Christ's death on the cross its final resolution. We will explore the meaning of that salvific event in terms of its atoning significance. The basic question is What happened at the cross?

Christ Suffered

The witness of the Scripture is consistent and clear: Christ suffered in a way and magnitude never experienced or ever to be experienced by any human being. Christians suffer for their faith (Rom. 8:18; 1 Peter 2:19, 20; 3:14), but they find in the suffering of Christ and the way He dealt with it an example to emulate (1 Peter 2:21; 4:1; cf. 2 Cor. 1:5, 6). The life of Christ in a world of sin was one of constant suffering as He observed and experienced the effects of sin and evil on humans and nature. He also endured the pressure of temptations brought upon Him by the enemy (Heb. 2:18) and as a result of His submission to the will of the Father (Heb. 5:8).

As the encounter between Christ and the forces of evil approached its climactic moment, He knew that it was necessary to "go to Jerusalem and suffer many things . . . , and that he must be killed" (Matt. 16:21). The suffering that culminated in His death also included being treated with contempt, that is to say, He was going to be regarded as nothing (Mark 9:12; Greek, *exoudeneō*, "treat with contempt/scorn") and "rejected" (Mark 8:31; Greek, *apodokimatsō*). The last verb implies that the Jewish leaders would scrutinize and declare Him useless, totally unworthy. Humans would devaluate Him (Isa. 53:3). The prophets of Israel had predicted His sufferings (1 Peter 1:11). Hebrews 2:9 summarizes the singularity of

Christ's suffering: "But we see Jesus, who was made a little lower than the angels, now crowned with glory and honor because he suffered [*pathema*] death, so that by the grace of God he might taste death for everyone." The passage begins with a reference to the moment of the Incarnation and to the glorification of the Son after His ascension. His exaltation was anchored in His suffering to the point of dying. But what made that deadly suffering unique was that He experienced it "for everyone." The magnitude of the suffering was incomprehensible.

The New Testament particularly associates the *pathema*/suffering of Christ with His sacrificial death (Heb. 9:26; 13:12). Peter states that He "suffered for sins once and for all, the just for the unjust, so that He might bring us to God" (see 1 Peter 3:18).[1] The Greek version of the Old Testament often uses the Greek phrase *peri hamartiōn*, translated "for sins," to refer to the sin offering. If Peter had that in mind, he was saying that Christ suffered on account of our sin as a sacrificial expiatory victim. This happened at the moment of His death on the cross, when His suffering reached unimaginable dimensions. The mission of Christ was to come to suffer and die for sinners, and He did it vicariously—"the just for the unjust."[2] Peter specifically states that Christ suffered in the flesh, i.e., as a human being (1 Peter 4:1). The incarnation, suffering, and death of Christ were inseparable from His mission. We need to explore the nature of that suffering.

Christ's Emotional and Spiritual Suffering

Shortly before His passion, Jesus said, "Now my heart is troubled, and what shall I say? 'Father, save me from this hour'? No, it was for this very reason that I came to this hour. Father, glorify your name!" (John 12:27, 28). The anticipation of His death on the cross terribly disturbed Jesus' inner being—He felt a natural disgust toward death. The verb *tarassō*, translated as "to be troubled," refers to inward turmoil, to mental and spiritual agitation, even confusion,[3] all in anticipation of an approaching extraordinary event.[4] In the case of Jesus the element of confusion was not present, because He had already made up His mind. He willingly embraced His destiny in fulfillment of the divine plan for the salvation of humanity. The experience that He anticipated was that of the cross interpreted in a unique way.

As Jesus approached Gethsemane His emotional state radically shifted from one of peace and rest to one of deep internal upheaval. An inner emotional disruption overtook Him and seriously threatened His very life. Jesus said to three of His disciples, "My soul is overwhelmed with sorrow [*perilupos*] to the point of death" (Mark 14:34). *Perilupos* refers to a state of deep sadness and grief and implies an inner struggle (cf. Mark 6:26; Luke 18:23). In the case of Jesus, His inner condition was so damaging that He considered it to be the threshold of death. He further described it as being "deeply distressed [*ekthambeō*] and troubled [*adēmoneō*]" (Mark 14:33). The verb *ekthambeō* depicts a state or condition characterized by intense emotional excitement caused by something unexpected or perplexing. For Jesus, the excitement was of a negative nature and probably designated a state of alarm or astonishment caused by not being able to understand the nature of the experience that He was going through. Jesus was "deeply distressed." The verb *adēmoneō* adds, in a more explicit way, the idea of anxiety—"to be in anxiety," "to be troubled" or "in distress."[5]

In Gethsemane Jesus' very being was going through a strong, disruptive, and life-threatening emotional storm that was already taking a toll on His body. He was ready to die, to surrender His life for undeserving sinners such as you and I. Luke says that He was "in anguish" (Luke 22:44). The Greek word translated "in anguish" (*agonias*) refers in general to "apprehensiveness of mind, especially when faced with impending ills, *distress, anguish.*"[6] It also expresses several important ideas difficult to combine in one English word. While it means "anxiety" or "fear," it is the anxiety that precedes and accompanies a conflict or struggle and that aims at being victorious.[7] The use in Luke suggests that Jesus was going through a fearful struggle and that He was anxiously confronting it so as to overcome. The level of the anxiety and the struggle was so intense that His life began to escape, as evidenced by the drops of sweatlike blood, the tangible expression of life, falling to the ground. Had it not been for an angel of God that came to strengthen Him, He would have probably died in Gethsemane (Luke 22:43).

In that distressing condition Jesus prayed. Although it may not be right to limit the description of the experience of prayer of Jesus recorded in Hebrews 5:7 to the one in Gethsemane, it does apply in a particular way to that moment in His life. There it declares: "During the days of Jesus' life on earth, he offered up prayers and petitions with loud cries and tears to the one who could save him from death, and he was heard because of his reverent submission." The terminology used indicates the emotional and spiritual intensity of the prayers and the dimension of suffering that the Lord went through. He was praying for deliverance from death, a significant detail in the case of Gethsemane. It also says that He "was heard." The answer to the prayer came on Sunday morning as a result of His "reverent submission" to the Father. Here again the connection with Gethsemane is clear.

Reason for Christ's Suffering

The Passion narratives in the Gospels do not explicitly tell us why Jesus went through such an excruciating experience in Gethsemane. At that point in His experience He faced no physical pain, as would be the case during the following hours. Consequently we have to conclude that the suffering was of an emotional and spiritual nature. What was causing it?

Experienced the judgment of the world. In John 12:31 Jesus associates the moment of His death with the world's judgment: "Now is the time for judgment on this world." The cross pronounced a verdict against the world not simply in the sense that humans and evil powers were guilty of crucifying the Son of God, but particularly in that the judgment of the world took place in the Son. He was "the Lamb of God, who takes away the sin of the world!" (John 1:29). That judgment aimed at the world's salvation: "For God did not send his Son into the world to condemn the world, but to save the world through him" (John 3:17). In other words, "the sentence of judgment passed on this world is endured by the One whom this world murders."[8] According to John, such a salvation is predicated on believing in Him (verse 18). When Christ was lifted up, God revealed His judgment against the world as well as the saving power of the cross (John 3:14; 12:32). It was the burden of that judgment that brought turmoil to the loving Savior. The Sinless One suffered on behalf of others, bearing the judgment against them.

The element of judgment is present in the image of the cup from which Jesus had to drink. While going through indescribable anguish and suffering, Jesus prayed, "My Father, if it is possible, may this cup be taken from me" (Matt. 26:39). Throughout the Old Testament the cup of the Lord figuratively refers to His saving power and to His judgment against unrepentant sinners. In the last case "the contents of the cup . . . are the judicial wrath of God [Jer. 25:15]. Like an intoxicating drink, this robs the one who must drink it of his senses, and causes him to stagger and fall, so that he cannot stand up again."[9] Jesus perceived His unavoidable death as directly related to the problem of sin and to God's attitude toward it. Otherwise, His experience of death would not have been unparalleled in its intensity and purpose.

Confronting the forces of evil. Jesus related the cross to the driving out of Satan: "Now the prince of this world will be driven out" (John 12:31). The Greek verb *ekkballō*, translated as "to drive out," is a technical term in the Gospels for the casting out of demons by Jesus (e.g., Matt. 8:16; 12:28; Mark 1:34, 39). His ministry was a constant victory over demonic powers. The Gospel of John contains no record of Jesus casting out demons, except in John 12:31. Since that passage does not mention the place from which Satan is cast out, it suggests that this was a direct encounter between Christ and Satan. Jesus went into the realm of darkness and personally confronted the power of evil, the prince of our world. In the Gospel of John darkness stands for the sphere of the world in rebellion against the light of God and against Christ, who is the light. Darkness characterizes the world under the control of the prince of the world (John 1:5, 9; 8:12). The New Testament unambiguously identifies Satan with the darkness of sin and death (e.g., Acts 26:18).

The cross was the hour when darkness reigned (Luke 22:53), and when Christ willingly entered its kingdom. In a sense it was Christ's descent to "hell."[10] He went into the realm of darkness by Himself, met the forces of evil head-on, and defeated them. Shortly before the Crucifixion Jesus announced to the disciples, "The prince of this world is coming. He has no hold on me" (John 14:30). Darkness had no hold on Jesus, and consequently, when He was lifted up on the cross, when He invaded the realm of darkness, He dethroned Satan (cf. Col. 2:15; Heb. 2:14). Thus when this intense conflict began in Gethsemane, Jesus experienced a profound emotional and spiritual upheaval.

Handed over to evil powers and death. The Bible uses the verb translated "to hand over, to give over, to deliver" (*paradidōmi*) to refer to what took place in the life of Christ from Gethsemane to His death on the cross. It is an important verb in that it throws light on the significance of the cross. In fact, it plays a vital role in the Passion narratives and in other parts of the New Testament.

Humans Handed Jesus Over: Very early the Gospel narratives identify Judas as the one who was going "to betray" or "hand over" Jesus (Matt. 10:4; Mark 3:19) to the Jewish leaders (Matt. 20:18), "into the hands of sinners" (Mark 14:41), or "into the hands of men" (Mark 9:31; Matt. 17:22). In fact, in the rest of the Passion narrative "to hand over" plays a major role. The Jewish leaders handed Jesus over to Pilate (Matt. 27:2; Mark 15:1), and he handed Him over to the Roman soldiers to be crucified (Mark 15:15; Matt. 27:26). Jesus had told the disciples that He was going to be handed over to the Gentiles and that they would "mock him, insult him, spit on him, flog him, and kill him" (Luke 18:32). Human beings orchestrated His death.

Jesus perceived in His being handed over through human instrumentalities something sinister. Behind Judas' evil action Jesus saw the activity of Satan, who had "entered Judas" shortly before he handed Him over to the Jewish authorities (Luke 22:3). One of the significant aspects of the verb *paradidōmi* is that it "signals delivery to a different sphere of power."[11] Here that sphere is the one of sin and demonic dominion (cf. 1 Cor. 5:5; 1 Tim. 1:10). The verb "designates the act whereby something or someone is transferred into the possession of another."[12] This is theologically very significant.

Jesus Handed Himself Over: The deliverance of Jesus to evil powers is not simply the result of human action, however. Paralleling the human and demonic evil act and intention, is a divine action and purpose. Jesus said to the Jews, "I lay down my life—only to take it up again. No one takes it from me, but I lay it down on my own accord. I have authority to lay it down and authority to take it up again. This command I received from my Father" (John 10:17, 18). The human and divine volitions coincided as they expressed themselves in their actions, while differing in their intention and purpose. Jesus, not humans, was in charge of what was happening: "I lay down my life for the sheep" (John 10:15); He came "to give his life as a ransom for many" (Mark 10:45); He "gave himself for me" (Gal. 2:20), for the church (Eph. 5:25). Finally, on the cross He "bowed his head and gave up his spirit" (John 19:30). Neither human nor satanic agencies took His life—He surrendered it voluntarily. Humans remained responsible for killing Him, but it was Jesus who willingly gave His life up.

God Handed Jesus Over: The Bible also shows that the Father had a direct role in handing Jesus over to the wicked and to the forces of evil. Jesus stated that in giving up His life, He was being obedient to the Father (John 10:18). In Romans 4:25 we find the use of the passive form of the verb, implying that God was the one who performed the action: "He [Christ] was delivered over to death for our sins." Obviously, the wicked did not intend to put Jesus to death *for our sins*. God was doing that for us. The divine passive is probably present in Mark 9:31: "The Son of Man is going to be betrayed [handed over] into the hands of men." In Scripture, when the subject of the verb for "to hand over" (*paradidōmi*) is God, it commonly connotes a negative result and presupposes a negative experience on the part of the object of the verb. Let me give some examples. Acts 7:24 has God handing over the Israelites who rebelled against Him to the consequences of their own sinfulness, or to the results of their sins. It is also the case in Romans 1:24, 26, 28, in which God hands the Gentiles over to their sinful ways. This is the way the wrath of God was being revealed against them (Rom. 1:18). The verb *paradidōmi* ("to hand over") carries in such cases the idea of divine judgment and could be rendered "hand over for judgment/punishment." The use is common in the Greek Old Testament (e.g., Isa. 34:2; Jer. 21:10; 32:28; Eze. 11:9).[13]

Such ideas appear to be in Paul's mind when he commented: "He who did not spare his own Son, but gave him up for us all—how will he not also, along with him, graciously give us all things?" (Rom. 8:32). The sentence "He who did not spare his own Son, but gave him up for us all" contains a profound thought that corresponds to what we found in the Gospel narrative. When the subject of the verb "to hand over" (*paradidōmi*) is God, it indicates that He was actively and intentionally transferring Christ to the power of sin and death, the realm of darkness (Rom. 4:25). The Old Testament located the ritually unclean in the sphere of uncleanness/death. The sacrificial victim was ritually transferred to that sphere on behalf of/in place of repentant sinners and experienced what the human beings should have experienced. Now it was Jesus that the Father handed over to that sphere, to die the way that all sinners should have died.

The language used by Paul in Romans 8:32 echoes the content of two passages from the Old Testament, and both support the position that God handed Jesus over to suffering and death. The first one is Genesis 22:16. At the last moment God provided a sacrificial victim as a substitute for Abraham's son. But in the case of Jesus, God did not spare Him but instead handed Him over as a sacrifice for our sins. The phrase "did not spare His Son" implies that the handing over was a painful experience for both the Father and the Son. The verb translated "spare" [*pheidomai*] means "to save from loss or damage."[14] Both ideas are present in our passage—

Jesus became poor for us and died for us. The second passage (LXX) is Isaiah 53:6. The text proclaimed that it was the Lord who delivered or handed the Servant over for the sins of the people. Notice that verse 12 explicitly states that the Servant handed over His own life unto death. We have already indicated that the Servant of the Lord in Isaiah was transferred to the sphere of death as a substitute for rebellious human beings who did not deserve divine mercy. The handing over of Jesus is at the heart of His redemptive work.

Jesus' Cry of Dereliction

The fact that Jesus was handed over to the powers of darkness suggests that He endured God's forsakenness. The experience was an expression of divine wrath, and consequently His suffering was intense beyond imagination and unbearable. In that context we should take seriously Jesus' cry: "My God, my God, why have you forsaken me?" (Mark 15:34; cf. Matt. 27:46). Mark introduces the shout—"Jesus cried out in a loud voice"—in the narrative after the statement "darkness came over the whole land" (Mark 15:33). The Gospel writers give no explicit interpretation of the darkness or the cry. Scripture itself becomes the context for understanding them. Darkness is primarily a symbol of divine judgment (e.g., Isa. 13:9-16; Amos 5:18-20; Jer. 13:16)[15] and probably serves in Matthew and Mark to indicate that the cross was the judgment of the world, an idea that we found in John.

Divine abandonment. It is at that dreadful hour that Jesus exclaimed, "Why have you forsaken me?" The least that we can say is that His question reveals the condition in which Jesus found Himself. Experiencing God's abandonment, He appropriated the words of the psalmist recorded in Psalm 22:1. In a sense He was enduring what humans often encounter in their lives—the apparent absence of God. Therefore Jesus was identifying Himself with the human condition, but more particularly with the suffering of the righteous.[16] In His case God's forsakenness was real and unique. As we have seen, in the context of the Passion narrative of the Gospels and the rest of the New Testament, God's abandonment of Jesus was the result of the Father's handing Him over to the sphere of sin and death for us. It was a real separation from God. The Righteous One, who knew no sin, was made sin for us (2 Cor. 5:21).

Divine love and judgment. God's judgment against sin—against the violation of His law—fell on His own Son. As we will show, we should never read this as God vindictively punishing His Son while the Son sought to persuade the Father to love us. They were not against each other, but rather were working together for our salvation. "Whatever happened on the cross in terms of 'God-forsakenness' was voluntarily accepted by both in the same holy love which made atonement necessary."[17] Ellen G. White adds: "God loved His Son in His humiliation. He loved Him most when the penalty for the transgression of His law fell on Him."[18] Yet Jesus experienced the eternal separation of sinners from God. It would be correct to conclude that *the sufferings of Christ had as their fundamental cause the anticipation and experience of His separation from the Father.*[19]

Deep thirst for God. The Gospel of John addresses this theological issue by reporting that on the cross Jesus said, "I am thirsty" (John 19:28). Obviously He was physically thirsty, but in the light of the meaning of His death in the New Testament, the statement is much more significant. It is probably an allusion to Psalm 22:16. "According to the psalm the righteous one has to bear both persecution and bodily deprivation of every kind; one recognizes in the experience of *being thirsty* the particular depth of human misery and exhaustion."[20] But the reference could also be to Psalm 42:1, 2, in which the psalmist describes the desire to enjoy the presence of God as a deep thirst for Him. Humans are characterized by thirst, and to them Jesus offered the living water (John 4:7-14; 7:37), promising them that whoever drinks of it will never thirst again (John 4:10-14). But now it was Jesus Himself who thirsted, and unfortunately His thirst could not be quenched. It was a thirst occasioned by feeling the intensity of His need for fellowship with God at a moment that He could not satisfy it. In a sense, "I am thirsty" is the equivalent of the cry of dereliction found in Matthew and Mark. It speaks of God's abandonment by using a different image.[21] The cry from the cross reveals the terror and desperation the Son faced on the cross in order for others to enjoy the water of life (John 19:34). It does not mean that He gave up on the Father. On the contrary, His faith remained intact in the midst of the struggle He faced. He experienced the abandonment, but at the same time He addressed the Father as "*My* God."

The Unity of the Two Natures and Divine Pathema/Suffering

We cannot separate the incarnation of the Son of God from His sacrificial death on the cross. In fact, as already indicated, the Incarnation made it possible for the Son of God to offer Himself for us. In order to explore the implications of that statement, we need to provide a brief summary of what we have already said about the Incarnation and add a few additional comments.

Implications of the union of the two natures. We have suggested, first, that the Incarnation was the union of the divine and the human in one person, the pre-existent Son of God. Second, each nature retained its own properties—the human was not divinized or the divine humanized, implying the presence of two wills in the incarnated Son of God. Third, the union of the two natures means that what the human nature went through, so did the divine, and that the human nature also experienced the manifestation of the power of the divine. What the divine nature perceived was the human emotions or needs.

Fourth, the Incarnation was the permanent union of the divine and the human in one person. The Son of God took our human nature to the very presence of God

(1 Tim. 2:5). Throughout eternity Jesus will remain human. The permanent union of the human and the divine in the person of Christ means that on the cross the two were inseparable. If we acknowledge that as a result of that eternal union the divine experienced what the human was going through, then one could suggest that the suffering of Jesus from Gethsemane to His death on the cross was experienced by both the human and divine natures, that is to say, by the totality of the person.

Before we develop those ideas, let me clarify an important issue. When dealing with this topic, we should be careful not to give the impression that Christ's divinity died on the cross. God is by definition immortal. The atonement required not the death of God but the death of rebellious sinful creatures. Through rebellion and sin they forfeited the gift of life and chose death—eternal death. It was *their* death as the penalty for sin that the Son of God took upon Himself as our substitute. On the cross human sinful nature was, so to speak, executed, making it possible for believers in Christ to die to sin and be reborn in the likeness of the Son of God.

Christ and divine *pathema*/suffering. Since God in His Son assumed responsibility for our sin, He voluntarily decided to experience in His own person *our* eternal penalty for sin. This would have required more than just knowing, through the Incarnation, how unrepentant sinners would feel as they face and experience the judgment of eternal death. We were not saved through human suffering but through divine *pathema*/suffering. Otherwise, God Himself would not have assumed responsibility for our sin. The Incarnation precisely made it possible for God to experience in His own person divine *pathema*/suffering for our sin. In order to have a glimpse at what was involved in that experience, we would have to know what was happening within the inter-Trinitarian relationships while Christ was dying on the cross. Here we are approaching the realm of human speculation, and caution is extremely important.

Two important statements from Ellen G. White will help us in exploring our topic. What she says finds support in the biblical understanding of the incarnation of the Son of God, particularly in the permanent union of the two natures. Here is the first: "In the darkest hour, when Christ was enduring the greatest suffering that Satan could bring to torture His humanity, His Father hid from Him His face of love, comfort, and pity. In this trial His heart broke. He cried, 'My God, my God, why hast thou forsaken me?'"[22] Several aspects of her statement need highlighting.

First, she located Christ in the realm of darkness, exactly what the New Testament indicated through the use of "to hand over." It implies increasing distance between the Father and the Son. He was going into the realm of darkness. Second, part of the suffering of the Son resulted from the torture inflicted upon His human nature by Satan. It involved not only His physical pain but also the constant temptations with which Satan assaulted Him. Third, yet another source of suffering even more intensely afflicted the Son—divine abandonment! The Father withdrew

His love, comfort, and pity from the Son. It does not mean that God did not love the Son, but that no mediator through whom divine love could reach Him was available. He was indeed separated from the Father on account of our sin. Fourth, the withdrawal of divine favor from Christ resulted in excruciating pain in the very being of the Son of God. That removal "ruptured" or, perhaps better, "suspended" the personal and loving fellowship that eternally existed between Father and Son. We cannot begin to imagine the magnitude of the intensity of the pain that Christ experienced on the cross. He knew the abandonment in the fullness of its abysmal depth, and it caused Him to cry out, wondering what was happening to the Father who had thus abandoned Him. Thus the divine Son of God experienced in His own being, as our substitute, the penalty for our sin—our eternal separation from God.

God's *pathema*/suffering. The second statement deals more directly with the question of suffering within the Godhead. "His [Christ's] soul was made an offering for sin. It was necessary for the awful darkness to gather about His soul because of the withdrawal of the Father's love and favor; for He was standing in the sinner's place, and this darkness every sinner must experience. The righteous One must suffer the condemnation and wrath of God, not in vindictiveness; for the heart of the Father yearned with great sorrow when His Son, the guiltless, was suffering the penalty of sin. This sundering of the divine powers will never again occur throughout the eternal ages."[23]

A few comments are in order. First, she interprets the death of Christ in terms of a sin offering, implying that it is substitutive and that it expiates sin. Second, she explicitly states that the handing over of Jesus to the realm of darkness was the result of the divine abandonment. The Father withdrew His love and favor from the Son. Third, she gives the reason for this: The Son was dying as the substitute for sinners. In other words, rebellious human beings should have experienced the withdrawal of God's love and favor, but He provided a substitute who went through it in their place. Fourth, the Son was suffering God's wrath and condemnation, but not vindictively. It was not that the Father, controlled by a spirit of revenge against the Son, rejoiced in inflicting pain on the Son. On the contrary, the Father never stopped loving His Son, even when He was dying for our sin. It was just that because He was bearing our sin that love could not reach Him.

Fifth, the Godhead suffered with the Son when He endured the penalty of sin. We know very little about the nature of divine *pathema*/suffering. The only suffering we have any experience and understanding of is our own. But we do know that "God suffered with His Son, *as the divine Being alone could suffer*, in order that the world might become reconciled to Him."[24] Such divine *pathema*/suffering had a direct connection to the withdrawal of the Father's love and favor from the Son. This is what Ellen G. White proceeded to develop.

Sixth, she describes the abandonment of the Son as a "sundering of the divine powers." The phrase "divine powers" refers to the members of the Godhead. She wrote that "there are three living persons of the heavenly trio; in the name of these three great powers—the Father, the Son, and the Holy Spirit—those who receive Christ by living faith are baptized."[25] *At the moment Christ was experiencing God's forsakenness on the cross, something extremely "painful" was happening to the Godhead.* I call it "divine *pathema*/suffering." There was a "sundering of the divine powers." "Sundering" does not simply mean "to separate"—it has the greater sense of "to break apart," implying willingness to pull apart what otherwise should have remained united. The thought expressed here is profound and difficult to grasp it fully. When Christ was hanging on the cross the Godhead was experiencing a "sundering," a "breaking apart"! *That was the price paid for our redemption, without which there would not have been a means of atonement for our sins. The eternal separation of sinful creatures from God was experienced by the Godhead as the exclusion of the Son from the love and fellowship of the other members of the Godhead.*

How was the sundering of the Godhead possible? Through the incarnation of the Son of God. The union of the human and divine natures of the Son of God was permanent; so when the human nature experienced separation from God as a result of sin, the divine also felt that separation from the Godhead at an infinitely higher level. Because of that separation, the human died. But since the divine could not die, it remained separated from the circle of love and favor of God in a dimension that we as human beings cannot comprehend. At this point the self-emptying (*kenosis*) of the Son of God reached unfathomable dimensions. The permanent nature of the Incarnation does not allow us to suggest that it was suspended when Christ was dying on the cross. I would suggest that the separation consisted of the exclusion of the Son from the interaction of love that lies at the core of the divine Persons, something impossible apart from the Incarnation. Such exclusion had to be inscrutably painful to all three members of the Godhead, not only to the Son.

The sundering of the Godhead—the divine *pathema*—was the penalty for the sins of the human race that God sacrificially experienced in order for us to be reunited to Him. It was possible through Christ, who as our substitute bore our sins and consequently was excluded from the circle of divine love and fellowship in our place. I would suggest that the suffering experienced by the Godhead surpassed the totality of the penalty for sin of the human race had it all perished. In other words, the divine *pathema* was more intense than even the magnitude of the eternal death of all sinners. Consequently, there is now an overabundance of divine grace (Rom. 5:21).

At this point some may raise a question: Does not this view sacrifice the unity of the Godhead in order to preserve the unity of the two natures in Christ? No, it does not. The fact that the abandonment of the Son meant the withdrawal of God's love and favor from the Son and its consequential divine *pathema*/suffering should not be interpreted to mean that the Divine Trio was no longer one. They mysteriously continue to be one, united around a common objective, namely, the salvation of sinners. There was no selfishness in them. What they were doing was exclusively for undeserving sinners at a heavy cost to the Godhead. There was also unity in suffering (divine *pathema*). It could be said, without blurring the distinctive roles of each member of the Godhead within the divine plan, that "God Himself was crucified with Christ; for Christ was one with the Father."[26] It is not simply that the person of Christ—His divine and human natures—suffered but that the other members of the Godhead also agonized with Him. We can safely say that on the cross "the omnipotent God suffered with His Son."[27] What is amazing is that "justice demanded the sufferings of man; but Christ rendered the sufferings of a God."[28] A loving sacrifice took place within the inter-Trinitarian relationships. That common experience within the Godhead preserved the unity of the three persons—it was unity in full divine self-giving.

Conclusion

On the cross the incarnated Son of God experienced the abandonment of God. The permanent union of the two natures made it possible for Him to bear our sin and guilt as our substitute. The divine abandonment resulted in the death of the human nature and, because of the union of the two natures, it caused an intense, indescribable suffering within the Godhead. The sundering of the Trinity—what I am calling "divine *pathema*." The Son of God was for a period of time excluded from the circle of Trinitarian love and fellowship but without destroying the unity of the Godhead. God indeed accepted responsibility for our sins through His Son. Such a sundering will never happen again.

---

[1] A number of Bible translations read "Christ died" (*apethanen*), instead of "suffered" (*epathen*). But on the basis of the manuscripts and the context of the passage, the best reading is "suffered."

[2] People used the preposition *huper*, translated "for," during the time of the New Testament to mean "in place of." This occasionally appears in the New Testament (see M. J. Harris, "Appendix: Prepositions and Theology in the Greek New Testament," in *New International Dictionary of New Testament Theology*, vol. 3, pp. 1196, 1197; and H. Patsch, "*Huper*, for, for the Sake of, in Place of," in *Exegetical Dictionary of the New Testament*, vol. 3, pp. 396, 397).

[3] F. W. Danker, *Greek-English Lexicon*, p. 990.

[4] H. Balz, "*Tarrasō*, Stir Up; Confuse, Trouble, Disturb," in *Exegetical Dictionary of the New Testament*, vol. 3, p. 335.

[5] Danker, p. 19.

[6] *Ibid.*, p. 17.

[7] Ethelbert Stauffer, "*Agonia*," *Theological Dictionary of the New Testament*, vol. 1, p. 140.

[8] George R. Beasley-Murray, *John* (Nashville: Thomas Nelson, 1999), p. 213.

[9] Leonhart Goppelt, "*Potērion*," in *Theological Dictionary of the New Testament*, vol. 6, p. 149.

[10] Cf. John R. W. Stott, *The Cross of Christ* (Downers Grove, Ill.: InterVarsity, 1986), p. 79.

[11] W. Popkes, *"Paradidōmi,* Hand Over; Pass On," in *Exegetical Dictionary of the New Testament*, vol. 3, p. 20.

[12] *Ibid.*, p. 18.

[13] See Peter G. Bolt, *The Cross From the Distance: Atonement in Mark's Gospel* (Downers Grove, Ill.: InterVarsity, 2004), p. 53.

[14] Danker, p. 1051.

[15] See Dale C. Allison, Jr., *Studies in Matthew: Interpretation Past and Present* (Grand Rapids: Baker, 2005), p. 97; Donald A. Hagner, *Matthew 14-28* (Dallas: Word, 1995), p. 844.

[16] See Rikk Watts, "The Psalms in Mark's Gospel," in *The Psalms in the New Testament*, eds. Steve Moyise and Maarten J. J. Menken (New York: T & T Clark, 2004), pp. 41-44; Maarten J. J. Menken, "The Psalms in Matthews's Gospel," *The Psalms in the New Testament*, pp. 78, 79.

[17] Stott, p. 151.

[18] Ellen G. White, "A Crucified and Risen Savior," *Signs of the Times*, July 12, 1899.

[19] Raoul Dederen comments: "In His death Jesus took our place, identifying Himself with sinners. From this identification, nevertheless, His soul shrank (Matt. 26:36-39, 42-44; Luke 22:41-44). This gives meaning to His cry of dereliction, 'My God, my God, why hast thou forsaken me?' (Mark 15:34). Why should Jesus be in an agony as He contemplated death? Was it fear of the torture He was undergoing? Many lesser than He have faced death calmly. What He shrank away from was not death as such, but the death that was the death of sinners, that death in which He, the Sinless One, would experience the horror of being separated from the Father, forsaken by Him. To this Paul seems to have referred when he wrote that God, 'for our sake *[hyper]*, . . . made him to be sin who knew no sin, so that in him we might become the righteousness of God' (2 Cor. 5:21). Christ became something which He had not been. It must mean that in an unfathomable way He took the place of those who would themselves otherwise suffer death. The apostle did not want to say that Jesus was a sinner, but he went as near as possible, conveying the thought that God regarded Him in the same way as He regarded sinners" (p. 177).

[20] H.-J. van der Minde, *"Dipsaō,* Thirst," in *Exegetical Dictionary of the New Testament*, vol. 1, p. 337.

[21] See Beasley-Murray, p. 351.

[22] E. G. White, *Manuscript Releases*, vol. 12, p. 407.

[23] *The Seventh-day Adventist Bible Commentary*, Ellen G. White Comments, vol. 7, p. 924.

[24] Ellen G. White, "Satan's Malignity Against Christ and His People," *Review and Herald*, Oct. 22, 1895. (Italics supplied.)

[25] Ellen G. White, *Evangelism* (Washington, D.C.: Review and Herald, 1946), p. 615. On page 617 she added, "We are to cooperate with the three highest powers in heaven—the Father, the Son, and the Holy Ghost—and these powers will work through us."

[26] Ellen G. White, "Christ's Victory Gained Through Pain and Death," *Signs of the Times*, Mar. 26, 1894.

[27] Ellen G. White, *The Upward Look* (Washington, D.C.: Review and Herald, 1982), p. 223.

[28] Ellen G. White, *The Faith I Live By* (Washington, D.C.: Review and Herald, 1958), p. 102.

11

ATONEMENT AND CHRIST'S MEDIATION
For Us Before the Father

The church members wanted a mural painted on one of the outside walls of the building. They obviously desired a religious motif. After some searching they found an artist, a painter who was a member of a congregation not far from theirs. After explaining to him what they had in mind, the man accepted the job. A few days later he brought a sketch of what he thought would be appropriate, and soon he slowly began to work on the wall of the church. After he traced the work of art on the wall, the colors soon began to appear. He was pouring his heart into it. Unfortunately the artist's physicians accidentally discovered that he had a terminal disease. It was so advanced that he died unexpectedly, leaving behind the uncompleted project. It is still there on the wall, unfinished. Had he completed it, it would have been a beautiful portrait of the face of Christ on the cross. Today when you look at the wall you see almost a shadow of an incomplete Christ.

Christ's atoning sacrifice on the cross, unlike that portrait, is finished. At the appropriate time Jesus proclaimed, "It is finished," and died. He voluntarily handed over His life to the Father. The conflict was over—He had been victorious. The sacrifice of Christ is a wonderful living canvas of redemption, forgiveness, and reconciliation for everyone to see. The saving power of that sacrifice includes His descent to the tomb, His resurrection and ascension, and His mediation before the Father. The redemptive efficacy of the death of Christ is available to us only through Christ's work of mediation.

From the Tomb the Throne of God

The Son of God went into the tomb. He had to remain there the apportioned time in accordance with the divine plan. Since the two natures are inseparable and yet distinct, we cannot say that death pulled them apart. Neither can we say that the human nature remained alive in the divine or that the divine literally died together with the human. Remember, the human was not divinized, and the divine was not humanized. We have to conclude that they remained united even in death (cf. Rom. 8:38, 39).

Christians have speculated concerning the experience of Christ while He was in the tomb. They based such conjecture to some extent on the doctrine of the immortality of the soul. What happened to the spirit/soul of Jesus while He was dead? Soon ancient theologians formulated the teaching of the descent of Christ to hell. According to it, He preached for three days to the souls of those incarcerated in hell, but such theologians never reached a clear consensus concerning what it was that He was specifically doing. The Bible does not support the idea of the immortality of the soul. When a person dies, he or she loses consciousness, and nothing survives in any form. This would mean that the human nature of Christ experienced death the same way we do—that is to say, no part of His human nature survived His physical death. At the moment of the resurrection Christ did not have to summon the soul or the spirit from heaven to join His dead body. Therefore our question is about the experience of Jesus' divine nature while He was in the grave. He certainly descended into the tomb (Matt. 12:40; Acts 2:24, 25; Eph. 4:9; Rev. 1:18).

Even though the Son of God was in the tomb as a result of taking our place, His divine nature rested, as suggested by His triumphant shout on the cross before He expired: "It is finished" (John 19:30). His work of redemption on earth had come to an end, and now the grave was a place of rest, not of conflict. His ultimate victory over evil powers and sin was assured. As divine rest followed Creation, now divine rest came after redemption or re-creation. The human nature rested in the sleep of death while the divine rested in the full assurance of a victory already obtained. The specific nature of that rest, however, remains a mystery to us.

We could also suggest that because of the union of the two natures, during the time the Son of God was in the tomb He looked in a unique way into the abysm of the nonbeing of sinful creatures—into the total darkness and unconsciousness of nonbeing. Since death is the penalty for sin, we could also suggest that the Son of God was in the tomb for three days as a result of assuming responsibility for our sin and guilt. His rest ended when the Father called on the Son to come out of the tomb through the power of His divine nature. At that moment His divine nature imparted life again to His human nature. He blasted open the tomb from inside out and left the door ajar for those who through faith in Him are willing to follow Him.

Atoning Sacrifice and Mediation

Christ finished the work that He came to do here on earth, and after the resurrection ascended to the throne of God—to the heavenly sanctuary. His mediation in no way overshadows or supplements His atoning sacrificial death. He finished His sacrificial work on the cross, but He is still working as king and priest in the heavenly sanctuary. One could even argue that "the simple resurrection from the dead in the sense of coming back to life would not sufficiently explain the salvific function of Christ; a real understanding of the salvific event comes only through the interpretation of the resurrection as exaltation and enthronement."[1] As high priest Jesus is now applying the benefits of His sacrifice to those who believe in Him.[2] Revelation 5:6-10 expresses the permanent efficacy of Christ's sacrifice through the symbol of a Lamb standing before the throne of God, looking "as if it had been slain." The work of redemption is not finished—only this Lamb can bring it to ultimate completion (verse 9). His sacrifice is the basis of His work as high priest and "his ascension-enthronement makes it possible for him to apply continually the benefits of his once-for-all sacrifice to the needs of his people (Heb. 7:25): it makes his sacrifice eternal in its effects (Heb. 9:12, 23-26; 10:12-14, 19ff.)."[3]

We can conclude that the atonement as a sacrificial event on the cross is finished, but that the atonement as a process leading to the cleansing of the heavenly temple and the whole cosmos from the impurity of sin remains yet unfinished. We have already demonstrated that the Old Testament applied the Hebrew term *kipper* ("to atone") not only to the sacrifice but also to the totality of the process that led to the final cleansing during the Day of Atonement. It has been correctly argued that in Hebrews the typological fulfillment of the Old Testament sacrificial system and of the priestly work in the person and work of Jesus indicates that "the atonement had not been completely made when Jesus died as a sacrifice on the cross. It is a process that finds analogous completion in the subsequent activity of Jesus in becoming a high priest and functioning as such. In addition to his crucifixion, that process includes his resurrection, his ascension, and coronation as Son of God and high priest 'after the order of Melchizedek' (Heb. 5:5, 6)."[4] The atonement as a process is an application and a manifestation of the atoning power of the sacrifice of Christ on the cross and occurs through Christ's ministry of mediation in the heavenly sanctuary (Heb. 7:25).

Christ's Mediation and God

Mediation implies distance that requires bridging. One could argue that the need for a mediator between God and His creation was always there from the moment that God created. In fact, creation was mediated through God's Word—He spoke, and it happened. The New Testament identifies that Word with Christ (John 1:1-3). The fall of humans into sin created a chasm between them and God that was impossible to span. Bridging it would occur only through an infinite sacrifice on the part of God Himself. In this case mediation took the form of that sacrifice. Consequently, the sacrifice of Christ is the most sublime expression of divine mediation. He stood between God and us and took upon Himself what was ours in order for us to receive and enjoy what was His.

Properly speaking, Christ's atoning mediation began at the moment of the

Incarnation. In His own person He brought together the human and the divine. He was the objective expression of the reconciliation of God and humans. His person was the place that the bridge between the two of them was located. With one hand He could reach to the heavens, and with the other He could reach down to us to restore our original state. Christ was unique because He, the only mediator, was born united to God. That union with God was universalized—that is to say, it became available to all—when on the cross He sacrificed it for us.

His mediation in the heavenly sanctuary cannot be separated from His mediation on the cross. We can be incorporated into His union with God through His mediation for us before the Father. His mediation means that there exists only one way of access to God. There is "one God and one mediator between God and men, the man Christ Jesus, who gave himself as a ransom for all" (1 Tim. 2:5, 6). The mediation of Christ is firmly anchored in His sacrificial mediation. His constant mediation before the Father means for humans that "salvation is found in no one else" (Acts 4:12). His uniqueness entitles Him to be our exclusive mediator.

But His mediation before the Father does not mean that He has to persuade the Father to accept us. Mediation presupposes that the Father is always lovingly disposed to restore us into fellowship through the Son. It also means that from the heavenly perspective the solution to the problem of sin is not yet consummated. Even Christians continue to exist tainted by sin and therefore in constant need of the sanctifying grace of God that reaches us through Christ. That grace freely flows from the Father, but it comes to us through Christ. At no point will we ever be able to claim independence from the mediation of Christ as we approach the Father. It is on account of His mediation that sin is no longer an obstacle to our access to God.

Christ's mediation before the Father is indispensable because the cosmic conflict still goes on. The forces of evil often try to limit our access to the benefits of the sacrifice of Christ. They point to our detestable condition in order to argue that if God should grant those benefits to us, it would reveal that divine justice is itself unreliable (cf. Zech. 3:1, 2; Job 1:6-11; Rev. 12:10). The mediation of Jesus before the Father and the angels grounds the reception of God's grace by sinful human beings on Christ's sacrificial death. It demonstrates that God can rightly justify sinners who by faith have accepted Christ as Savior and Lord (cf. Rom. 3:25, 26).

The mediation of Christ is indispensable in that without it the Father would not have sent the Holy Spirit to us. Obviously we should not interpret that fact as suggesting an initial lack of desire on God's part to send the Spirit. The concern was finding the proper way to fulfill a divine intent. Once Christ offered Himself as a sacrifice and ascended to the Father, there was a Mediator through whom the Spirit would be sent to the world and particularly to the church. Jesus informed the disciples that at the beginning of His mediation, after His ascension, His first request to the Father would be to send them the Spirit (John 14:15). Then at Pentecost the dis-

ciples received the outpouring of the Spirit and understood it to mean that Christ
had begun His work of mediation (Acts 2:33).

Mediation of Christ and Common Grace

As soon as Adam and Eve sinned Christ became their mediator, making the
benefits of His future atoning sacrifice to them. He was the Lamb of God "slain
from the creation of the world" (Rev. 13:8). Through Christ's sacrifice and mediation grace now encircled the planet.[5] That sphere of grace made it possible for God
to continue to communicate with humans through Christ, calling us to salvation.
Christian theology usually refers to such grace as "common grace," the demonstration of God's concern for His undeserving creation. This grace benefits not only the
natural world but particularly human beings, and does not take into consideration
whether or not they actually serve the Lord. But such common grace is not considered to be salvific, that is to say, receiving its benefits does not mean that we have
been saved or that we are growing in holiness. What, then, is the purpose of this
work of Christ and how does it manifest itself?

Preserve and sustain nature and life. As a result of the sacrifice and mediation of Christ, God has not abandoned our world but continues to sustain it. The
psalmist says: "The Lord is good to all; he has compassion on all he has made" (Ps.
145:9). His mercy knows no limits. God's compassion expresses itself in His regular and unfailing maintenance of the world. Job 37:13 states that "he brings clouds
to . . . water his earth and show his love." The way the Lord provides for the sus-
tenance of the earth is a revelation of His love: "You care for the land and water it;
you enrich it abundantly" (Ps. 65:9).

If sin threatens one particular element of God's creation in a direct way, it is
the mysterious phenomenon of life on our planet. Out of His gracious love mediated to us through Christ, God has preserved the life He created in spite of its contamination with sin. Paul says: "For in him we live and move and have our being"
(Acts 17:28). This is the sphere of His grace made possible through the work of mediation of Christ. Again the psalmist adds: "O Lord, you preserve both man and
beast. How priceless is your unfailing love!" (Ps. 36:6, 7). The verb translated "preserve" is *yāshaᶜ*. In this case it means "to save, to help." The word "priceless"
comes from a root whose meaning is "scarce, rare" (*yāqār*; cf. 1 Sam. 3:1). It is
used to refer to gemstones because they are rare. From there it developed the meaning "precious, valuable." God's love is like a precious stone, but contrary to it, His
love is not rare or scarce. One can see and experience it constantly in the preservation of human and animal life on the planet. Life does not continue as the result of
mechanical laws working independently of God: "The physical organism of man is
under the supervision of God, but it is not like a clock, which is set in operation,
and must go of itself. The heart beats, pulse succeeds pulse, breath succeeds breath,

but the entire being is under the supervision of God. . . . Each heartbeat, each breath, is the inspiration of Him who breathed into the nostrils of Adam the breath of life—the inspiration of the ever-present God, the great I AM."[6]

Provision for temporal needs. In order to preserve human life on the planet, God had to provide for the basic life-sustaining needs of His creatures—again the result of the sacrifice and mediation of Christ for us. Paul and Barnabas said to a group of pagans, "He [God] has shown kindness by giving you rain from heaven and crops in their seasons; he provides you with plenty of food and fills your hearts with joy" (Acts 14:17). It is He who "makes grass grow for the cattle and plants for man to cultivate—bringing forth food from the earth" (Ps. 104:14). Even the lions "seek their food from God" (verse 21). One more passage from Psalms: "You care for the land and water it; you enrich it abundantly. The streams of God are filled with water to provide the people with grain, for so you have ordained it" (Ps. 65:9). All of this is totally undeserved by His creatures and is an expression of God's loving grace mediated through Christ. Our God "causes his sun to rise on the evil and the good, and sends rain on the righteous and the unrighteous" (Matt. 5:45). He is "kind to the ungrateful and wicked" (Luke 6:35).

Social impact. God's common grace mediated through Christ has a social impact. The violence and suffering that we witness make it difficult for some to believe that God actively controls the forces of evil on our planet. But the evil we see is significantly small compared to what it would be if God were to deliver the planet fully into the hands of evil powers. In restraining the increase of evil and violence, God wants to employ the legal systems of the nations (Rom. 13:3, 4, 6). He uses those powers to limit the inroads of evil in society, making it possible for us to live in relative peace in order to fulfill our mission.

God holds back the impact of the agencies of evil on the nations until the appointed time, when they will play their role in God's plan (cf. 2 Thess. 2:6, 7). It is what the books of Daniel and Revelation show through the time prophecies recorded in them. In that way those books point to the fact that God is the Lord of history. That philosophy of history rests on the fact that the most significant event in our history took place on Calvary. Without it, history would lack purpose and direction, and without it the nations of the earth would be heading, together with every human being, to total extinction.

The Scriptures testify that God is involved in human history, leading it to a particular goal—the establishment of the His kingdom on earth. At the present time His hand remains hidden in the mystery of His providential acts, but He is fully active among us. Daniel recognized God's unseen presence in history when he declared: "He changes times and seasons; he set up kings and deposes them" (Dan. 2:21). God has not relinquished His control over the nations of the earth. He works in the hearts of leaders, quietly but effectively, to accomplish His purpose (Ezra

1:1). The fall of wicked nations happens under the control of our God. Concerning Babylon, He announced: "I will stir up and bring against Babylon an alliance of great nations from the land of the north. They will take up their positions against her, and from the north she will be captured" (Jer. 50:9; cf. 51:11). The prophecies against the nations in the Old Testament prophetic books provide clear evidence to the fact that God is the one who rules over the earth. The political situation of the world would be in a much more chaotic condition were it not for the fact that God is still active in it. That divine intervention is possible because all the nations of the earth belong to our Lord on account of the sacrifice of Christ.

Restraining human sinfulness. It is in the human heart that the most ferocious battles between God and humanity rage. The heart is the citadel of evil or good. As a result of the mediation of Christ, the Spirit works in the human heart, restricting its total corruption. At times God stops humans from committing certain sins. King Abimelech claimed before God to be innocent of any sin and was ready to question God's justice in punishing him. God said to him, "Yes, I know you did this with a clear conscience, and so I have kept you from sinning against me. That is why I did not let you touch [Sarah]" (Gen. 20:6). Whatever good is left in the human heart is the work of God restraining its sinfulness. The heart is not good by nature (James 1:17).

Source of wisdom and knowledge. We must attribute the continuing developments in the sciences, the arts, and technology to the presence of God among us: "He gives wisdom to the wise and knowledge to the discerning. He reveals deep and hidden things" (Dan. 2:21, 22). God fills people with "skill, ability and knowledge in all kinds of crafts" (Ex. 31:3). If the human mind is still able to think rationally, if human beings are still interested in understanding themselves and the world around them, if we are still searching for meaning, it is because God is preserving His image in us. He is able to do that for us without compromising the holiness of His character because of His work for us through Christ.

Drawing all to Christ. As a result of this common grace the Spirit of the Lord is fully active on our planet, pointing and leading individuals to the cross as the only means of salvation. Jesus said to the disciples that after His departure He was going to send them the Spirit, and that He will "convict the world concerning sin and righteousness and judgment" (John 16:8, NASB). The Greek term translated "convict" is *elegchō*, which means "to rebuke, blame, correct, punish," "show someone his or her fault," or "convince someone of his or her fault or error." The rebuke aims at the improvement of the person. This is common grace. The Spirit seeks to convince every person of sin, righteousness, and judgment. His work leaves individuals in a state of guilt, making them aware of their alienation from God and their sinfulness. He seeks to help human beings realize that they are lost in the universe and without God. It is then that He points to the cross as the only way out of the human predicament. Without this work of the Spirit the cross becomes ineffective in itself. But it is precisely because of the cross that the Spirit is active in the world, directing sinners to the effectiveness of the cross for their salvation. All the good gifts and blessings that humans enjoy from God have the purpose of leading them through the Spirit to the cross of Calvary (Rom. 2:4).

Mediation and the Christian Life

Those who have put their faith in Christ are in constant need of the work of mediation of Christ before the Father. Paul proclaimed that "Christ Jesus who died—more than that, who was raised to life—is at the right hand of God and is also interceding for us" (Rom. 8:34). The phrase "for us" affirms that Christ mediates on behalf of believers. The mediation of Christ "for us" presupposes that sin is still a menace for believers in that it could damage their relationship with the Lord. The possibility of postbaptismal sin is real and constant, and whenever it occurs God does not ignore it. That fact makes the role of Christ as our mediator before the Father an indispensable element in the Christian life. John was fully aware of that situation: "My dear children, I write this to you so that you will not sin. But if anybody does sin, we have one who speaks to the Father in our defense—Jesus Christ the Righteous One" (1 John 2:1). He goes on to suggest that the forgiveness of sin through the effectiveness of the mediation of Christ before the Father is assured to all—believers and nonbelievers—because "he is the atoning sacrifice for our sins, and not only for ours but also for the sins of the whole world" (verse 2). God exclusively mediates His forgiveness to us through Christ (Eph. 4:32).

Christians were sanctified through the blood of Christ at the moment of conversion (e.g., Heb. 10:29), but Christ continues to establish their hearts in holiness (1 Thess. 3:13). In fact, Scripture exhorts them to be holy because God is holy (1 Peter 1:15, 16). But the exhortation is cemented in the conviction that Christ mediates holiness to us through His work in the heavenly sanctuary. Scripture urges believers to "approach the throne of grace with confidence, that we may receive mercy and find grace to help us in our time of need" (Heb. 4:16). Christians will face such "[times] of need," but through the heavenly high priest they will obtain the assistance they require to face those difficult moments. Our Savior has not abandoned us to struggle alone in our Christian life. He was the Abandoned One, and consequently He will never let us go, but will be with us always to the very end (Matt. 28:20).

Conclusion

The work of atonement of Christ includes His death, resurrection, ascension, and His work of mediation before the Father. We should never limit the atonement to the sacrificial act, but should interpret it as a process. The atoning power of the sacrifice of Christ is now being applied to believers through the mediation of the Son of God. That mediation made it possible for humans to enjoy the presence of the Spirit on our planet and all the many blessings that He brings to all, believers as well as nonbelievers. The "common grace" mediated through Christ in the work of the Spirit aims at moving the human heart to find in Christ their Savior. "Sanctifying/saving grace" is the work of the Spirit in the heart of those who surrendered their lives to Christ. Even for them the mediation of Christ in the heavenly sanctuary continues to be indispensable. Through it they graciously receive forgiveness for postbaptismal sins, continue to grow in grace, and are sustained as they confront trials and temptations in the Christian journey.

---

[1] Martin Hengel, *Studies in Early Christology* (Edinburgh: T & T Clark, 1995), p. 153. Commenting on the use of the term *leitourgos* ("minister") in Hebrews 8:2, David J. MacLeod says that it is "drawing attention to the fact that though His sacrificial work is finished, there is a ministry that continues" ("The Present Work of Christ in Hebrews," *Bibliotheca Sacra* 148 [1991]: 187). The thought had already been expressed by Donald Guthrie, *The Letter to the Hebrews: An Introduction and Commentary* (Grand Rapids: Eerdmans, 1983), p. 171.

[2] Cf. David Peterson, *Hebrews and Perfection: An Examination of the Concept of Perfection in the "Epistle to the Hebrews"* (Cambridge: Cambridge University Press, 1982), p. 115, who writes, "The emphasis on the finished nature of his atoning work, particularly in 10:11ff. means that believers are being challenged to enjoy the ongoing benefits of that work (10:19ff.) and the image of the intercessor is used to emphasize Christ's willingness and ability to go on applying those benefits (cf. 12:24)." The statement is in principle correct, but it weakens the intercessory work of Christ by interpreting it as an "image." Hebrews identifies Jesus as a mediator through whom the new covenant was put into effect and as our mediator in heaven. Hence "the forgiveness once and for all secured has its application in the essential help it provides to 'the children' on the difficult path to glory" (M. A. Seifrid, "Death of Christ," in *Dictionary of the Later New Testament and Its Developments*, p. 275).

[3] Peterson, p. 119.

[4] John McRay, *Paul: His Life and Teaching* (Grand Rapids: Baker Academic, 2003), p. 324. Some years ago J. G. Davies expressed the same idea on page 66 of *He Ascended into Heaven: A Study in the History of Doctrine* (New York: Association Press, 1958) when he wrote: "By accomplishing this offering Christ made atonement, and this act is a process: the dying, by which His blood is outpoured; the rising, by which 'God brings again from the dead the great shepherd of the sheep with the blood of the eternal covenant' [Heb 13:20], and the ascending, by which He enters into heaven itself with the blood 'now to appear before the face of God for us' [Heb. 9:24]." See also Hengel, p. 160.

[5] Ellen G. White has expressed it well: "In the matchless gift of His Son, God has encircled the whole world with an atmosphere of grace as real as the air which circulates around the globe. All who chose to breathe this life-giving atmosphere will live and grow up to the stature of men and women in Christ Jesus" (*Steps to Christ* [Mountain View, Calif.: Pacific Press, 1956], p. 68).

[6] Ellen G. White, *Medical Ministry* (Mountain View, Calif.: Pacific Press, 1932), p. 9.

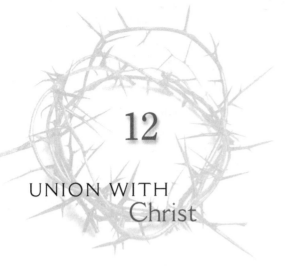

12

UNION WITH Christ

Christ has performed a work of salvation for us independent and outside of us. Through Him God removed the barrier of sin that hindered the reconciliation of humanity with Him. At the cross Christ took upon Himself our sin and its penalty without asking us whether or not we wanted Him to do that for us. He died in place of sinners before we were willing to confess Him as Savior and Lord. In dying for all, God counted His death as the penalty for the death of all. He paid with His own life for our redemption before we realized that we were slaves of sin, death, and evil powers. That objective work of Christ revealed the justice and sacrificial love of God for undeserving human beings to the world not only on earth but to the rest of the universe. Yet that objective work of Christ has no saving power for us as individuals unless we appropriate it through faith in Him.

God's Initiative in Our Appropriation of Salvation

The saving work of Christ includes the activity of the Spirit in the human heart calling us as sinners to see in Christ God's redemptive activity for us. The appropriation of the redemption that Christ obtained is directly related to His work as mediator before the Father and to the work of the Spirit in the human heart. As indicated in the previous chapter, through Christ's mediation God's grace flowed down to all human beings in what we have called common grace. It is also part of the objective work of Christ for us. Grace was there, working for us before we understood it and much less accepted it. But that grace, through the work of the Spirit, has been leading humans to Christ as their Savior. In the midst of our rebellion the Spirit was working in our hearts, wooing us and inviting us to look at the cross— at our Substitute.

God not only included in His plan the mediation of Christ and the work of the Spirit; He also involved other human beings. Those who surrender their hearts to the soothing influence of the Spirit, allowing Him to sanctify them, become the

Spirit's instruments to proclaim God's work in Christ. This is the ministry of reconciliation, about which we have already spoken. Now others hear the voice of the Spirit through the voices of sanctified human beings who have accepted the free gift of salvation through Christ. They become His ambassadors in a world at war with God, announcing that the death of the Son of God has removed the barrier—sin—hindering a peaceful relationship with God. The Lord took the initiative and instituted the ministry of reconciliation for the salvation of sinners.

Call and Election

The movement toward the personal appropriation of salvation begins with the *divine call* to believe in Christ as Savior and to submit humbly to Him as Lord. It is fundamentally a summons to salvation and faith in Christ. God is the one who calls (1 Peter 1:15; 1 Thess. 5:24), and His calling is based on His free will and purpose, that is to say, it is not motivated by our goodness or works, and consequently it is solely the result of God's grace toward us (Gal. 1:6). Universal, it includes both Jews and Gentiles (Rom. 9:24) and reaches them through the gospel of salvation (2 Thess. 2:14). A call "out of darkness into his [God's] wonderful light" (1 Peter 2:9), it leads to peace (1 Cor. 7:15), to freedom (Gal. 5:13), to fellowship with Christ (1 Cor. 1:9), to sharing in His glory (2 Thess. 2:14), to holiness (1 Thess. 4:7; 1 Cor. 1:2), to becoming part of His people, the church (Col. 3:15; cf. 1 Thess. 2:12), to eternal life (1 Tim. 6:12), and to the hope of a glorious inheritance (Eph. 1:18). What distinguishes Christians from other human beings is that they have heard the call and accepted it (1 Cor. 1:2), thus identifying themselves as those called by God (Rom. 1:6; 9:24). In that sense they have appropriated the gift of salvation divinely offered to them. The acceptance of the call leads to justification by faith in Christ (Rom. 8:30), which presuppose repentance and confession of sins.

Election cannot be separated from the divine call to salvation and service. In Scripture election is God's free act of choosing from among a group. Some biblical examples are His election of Israel from among the nations of the earth (Deut. 7:6, 7), the appointing of Christ to be our Savior (Luke 9:35), and the selection of Paul as a missionary to the Gentiles (Acts 9:15). In His sovereign will God chooses some individuals to perform a particular task (Rom. 9:14-24). When the New Testament uses the word "election" theologically, it always refers to those who have placed their faith in Christ, and whom God has chosen for a particular role or mission. It could designate both the individual (Acts 1:24) and the church (Titus 1:1; 1 Peter 1:1). The Bible does not know anything about double predestination—God choosing some for salvation and others for perdition.

Also the Bible does not teach the universal election of every individual to salvation independent of a faith relationship with the Lord. We do find an element of universality, but it is understood as meaning that through the preaching of the gospel and the work of the Spirit God is choosing not only Jews but also Gentiles (1 Thess. 1:4). Jesus said: "For many are invited, but few are chosen" (Matt. 22:14). Here the calling and the election stand together, and those who have been chosen are identified as those who have accepted the divine call. God has been doing all He can to move all to accept the call and be saved (1 Tim. 2:4).

Our election is an expression of divine grace, something Paul had in mind when he wrote that God "chose us in him [Christ] before the creation of the world" (Eph. 1:4). The divine decision took place before we existed—prior to the creation of the world—and consequently it was part of the divine mystery for the salvation of sinners.[1] The text speaks of only the preexistence of Christ. It is the decision to elect us in Christ that happened before the creation of the world.[2] We are in reality talking about God's pre-Creation plan for us—what He had predetermined to do on behalf of His people. Heaven then revealed that plan to us in the person of Christ and in Him gave us the gift of salvation (1 Tim. 1:9, 10). The phrase "granted/given to us in Christ" "signifies that it is brought to us in Christ's person and work."[3]

According to Ephesians 1:3, 4, God, in accordance with His purpose and sovereign will, predetermined that our election will take place exclusively "in Christ." That is an important phrase to which we shall return, but for now it means that our election is a reality *through* and *in union* with Christ. And that is possible because He is the Elect One (Luke 9:35; 1 Peter 2:4), and as such He is the person, the sphere, within which our election occurs. We are elected/chosen only in the Chosen One—never outside or apart from Him. We could conclude that "those who respond to the drawing of Christ, through the sovereign mercy of God, are elected to be saved as the obedient children of God. Upon them is manifested the free grace of God, the great love wherewith He hath loved us. The Father sets His love upon His elect people, who live in the midst of men, because they accept the redemption which Christ has purchased for them by His own precious blood."[4] Such an election manifests itself in a "holy and blameless" life (Eph. 1:4). In fact, election is being chosen not simply for salvation but for a holy life. The one cannot be separated from the other without robbing election of its meaning and content. The appropriation of the saving power of the atoning death of Christ has a major impact in the life of the believer.

United to Christ

The grace of God aims at uniting repentant sinners to Christ in order for them to receive the full benefits of His saving death. On the cross Christ died as our substitute, but in our union with Him we join Him as Savior and Lord. Nowhere in the New Testament do we read about believers dying "in Christ," that is to say, in union with Him. He died alone on the cross—abandoned by all, including the Father. Our union with Christ designates the experience of the new creature and presupposes the death of the old self. Such union with Him is the subjective experience of the atonement.

"In Christ."[5] The New Testament specifically expresses the idea of union with Christ through the phrases "in Christ," "in Him," and "in the Lord." The difference in meaning among them is insignificant, with the exception that "in the Lord" appears to emphasize more than the other two the idea of His lordship. In order to simplify matters, in what follows we will use the more common phrase "in Christ," even in cases in which the text employs "in Him/in the Lord." In the phrase the preposition "in" (Greek *en*) could express the idea of instrumentality ("through") or locality ("in," "in the sphere of").

God and "In Christ": A number of passages inform us that God does something for us "in Christ." For instance, it is in Christ that God grants us grace (Eph. 1:6; 2:7; 2 Tim. 1:9), the call (Phil. 3:14; 1 Cor. 7:22), election (Eph. 1:4, 11), forgiveness (Eph. 4:32), justification (Gal. 2:17; cf. 2 Cor. 5:21), reconciliation (2 Cor. 5:19), redemption (Eph. 1:7), sanctification (1 Cor. 1:2), blessings (Eph. 1:3; Gal. 3:14), eternal life (Rom. 6:22), and glorification (2 Thess. 1:12). It is also God who in Christ gives us freedom (Gal. 2:4) and victory (2 Cor. 2:14), strengthens and encourages us (Phil. 4:13; 2:1), is accessible to us (Eph. 3:12), and seats us in heavenly places. The implication of Paul's use of the phrase "in Christ" is that God has been and is still fully active in Christ. It is through Christ and in union with Christ that the Father has granted us so many gifts. Christ is the sphere of divine activity on behalf of humans—the "place" where God does many wonderful things for us and where there is no condemnation for us (Rom. 8:2).

Believers Are "In Christ": While God was active in Christ for our salvation, believers are also in Christ enjoying the benefits and responsibilities of that salvation. Here the phrase describes the sphere of existence of those who have put their faith in Him. In Christ they are new creatures (2 Cor. 5:17), find the righteousness that is by faith (Phil. 3:9), and are holy and faithful (Eph. 1:1; Phil. 1:1; 4:12; Col. 1:2). They died to sin and are now alive to God in Christ (Rom. 6:11), living a holy life in Him (2 Tim. 3:12). Paul refers to believers as those who "are in Christ Jesus" (1 Cor. 1:30). They are all brothers only in Christ (Phil. 1:14; Philemon 16).

Since Christ determines the existence of believers, they rejoice (Phil. 3:1; 4:4), glory (1 Cor. 15:31; Phil. 3:10), boast (1 Cor. 1:31), labor (1 Cor. 15:58; Rom. 16:12), and hope in Him (1 Cor. 15:19; Eph. 1:12). They have placed their faith in Him (Gal. 5:6) and lived their life in Him (Col. 2:6, 7) totally oriented and determined by Him (1 Cor. 4:17). In fact, the union of believers to Christ is so intimate and all-encompassing that to be "in Christ" is another way of saying that a person is a Christian. When Paul says that Andronicus and Junia "were in Christ before I was," he means that they became Christians before he was converted. The phrase "infants in Christ" indicates immature Christians (1 Cor. 3:1), and to be "wise in Christ" (1 Cor. 4:10) is the equivalent of being a wise Christian. In those cases we should keep in mind that the phrase "in Christ" still retains the idea of a personal union with Christ that determines the quality of the life of the Christian.

Unity of Believers "In Christ": There is a community of believers that is collectively in Christ, a union reflected in their relationship with each other. What happened is that "in Christ we who are many form one body, and each member belongs to all the others" (Rom. 12:5). Paul describes each local congregation as being in Christ (Gal. 1:22; 1 Thess. 2:14). The church is like a building being constructed in Christ in whom church members are also "being built together to become a dwelling in which God lives by his Spirit" (Eph. 2:22). Within this collectivity of believers "there is neither Jew nor Greek, slave nor free, male nor female, for you are all one in Christ Jesus" (Gal. 3:28). What determines how they relate to each other are not the cultural, social, religious, and gender distinctions, but their union with the resurrected Lord. Common to them and of fundamental importance is the fact that they are all in Christ. It determines everything that takes place within the congregation. Children are to obey their parents in the Lord (Eph. 6:1), women and men find interdependence in the Lord (1 Cor. 11:11), and those who get married should marry in Christ, i.e. with a believer (1 Cor. 7:39).

The common union with Christ that believers enjoy impacts the totality of the life of the congregation. Its members send greetings to each other in Christ (Rom. 16:22; 1 Cor. 16:19), and exhort, urge, and speak to each other in Christ (Eph. 4:17; 1 Thess. 4:1; 1 Cor. 12:19). Leaders exercise their authority within that same spiritual union. They are to officiate over the congregation "in the Lord" (1 Thess. 5:12), and they are to give their orders and commands in Christ (2 Thess. 3:12). Those who minister refer to each other as fellow workers/servants "in the Lord" (Rom. 16:3, 9; Col. 4:7). In those cases Paul uses the phrase "in Christ/the Lord/Him" to define "how believers were to live under Christ's saving lordship" and consequently the phrases "became a vehicle for Paul to describe the life of faith under Christ's lordship in a world where other powers and temptations were present. To act 'in Christ' is to act in faith and obedience in the face of false alternatives."[6]

Cosmic Significance of "In Christ": The phrase takes us beyond the confines of the church, and even of the world, into the immensity of the universe. Paul now describes the whole cosmos as being "in Christ" (Col. 1:16). Many English versions read "through Christ," giving to the preposition "in" a possible instrumental significance. But we should not totally exclude the idea of union with Christ. He brought into existence a cosmos in perfect union and harmony with God. It was created under His Lordship and through His power—"in him" "all things hold together" (verse 17). He is at the center of the cosmos, providing it stability, consistency, and permanency. Sin threatened that harmony, but Christ has restored it.

Our discussion of "in Christ," and similar phrases, indicates that they do not refer to a mystical union with Christ in which believers are detached from the experiences of their daily life. On the contrary, the phrase designates the realm or sphere of existence within which believers live their Christian faith. The saving work and the lordship of Christ conditions and determines their whole life. The New Testament contrasts that view of the Christian life to a realm of existence "in the flesh," characterized by worldly existence (e.g., Phil. 3:3; 1:21, 22; Rom. 8:8, 9; 1 Tim. 3:16; Philemon 16).[7] "In Christ" refers to an intimate relationship with the risen Savior that constantly acknowledges His lordship in the life of the believer and in the church. It proclaims that the existential center of humanity, lost through the fall into sin, has been restored through and in Christ.

Two humanities. We still need to clarify a little more how it is possible for humans to be in Christ. Our starting point should probably be the biblical teaching of the two Adams, from whom originated two humanities. Paul speaks of a "first man/Adam" and a "last/second man/Adam" (1 Cor. 15:45, 47). Humans belong by nature to the first Adam—that is to say, they are part of the fallen human race whose head or father was Adam. They are born "in Adam" in the sense that they belong to or are inexorably united to sinful humanity, and as such their fate is fixed: "In Adam all die" (verse 22). The phrase "in Adam" does not refer to the presence of every human being "in Adam"—a type of corporate or mystical presence in him—but to the spiritual condition in which human beings find themselves as a result of the first Adam's fall. They have been unable to escape from the sphere of sin that he brought into existence.

The New Testament compares and contrasts the two Adams in order to demonstrate that the fate of humans is no longer determined by being "in Adam," but by being or not being "in Christ." We will examine the main elements of that contrast. First, Scripture calls each Adam a "son of God" (Luke 3:38, 22). Adam is son of God through creation, while Christ, the second Adam, is the eternal Son of God. Second, the first Adam "was of the dust of the earth," but the second Adam is "from heaven," pointing to His place of origin (1 Cor. 15:47). Third, the first Adam "became a living being" (verse 45)—in other words, he did not have life in himself. He received it from God. But the second Adam is "a life-giving spirit" (verse 45). He has life in Himself and can give and has given life to others. Fourth, the first Adam chose *disobedience* to or transgression of God's law in an act of rebellion against Him (Rom. 5:19). Christ came and never broke up His relationship with the Father. He was perfectly *obedient* to God.

Fifth, the first Adam brought *sin* into the world (verse 12), but Christ, as the second Adam, brought the gift that consists of an overabundance of *grace* for all who receive it (verses 15, 17). Sixth, it was through Adam that *death* entered the world, and it has inexorably come "to all men" (Rom. 5:12; 1 Cor. 15:21). In fact, the reign of sin is grounded in the reality that all die. Hence, what we get from Adam is physical and spiritual death, not his personal sin, in which we did not participate. Christ brought to the human race eternal *life* (Rom. 5:21). Seventh, the result of the transgression of Adam was a judgment of *condemnation* against sinful humanity (verses 16, 18). Through the one act of righteousness the second Adam brought *justification* to sinful human beings (verse 16)—a justification "that brings life for all men" (verses 18, 21).

Those contrasts reveal that the first Adam originated a human family separated from God, spiritually dead. As a result of his sin, death awaits all. Their condition made it impossible for humans to overcome the power of sin in their lives, and consequently sin became inevitable. Christ brought into existence in His own person a human family united to God. He has given to those who belong to Him new life, and consequently sin is no longer their inevitable fate. They are alive in Him, and sin no longer reigns over them.

Members of the new humanity. As indicated, humans are born into Adam's family through natural birth. In order to be part of the family of the second Adam we also need to be born into it. To those who believed in the name of Jesus, "he gave the right to become children of God—children born not of natural descent, nor of human decision or a husband's will, but born of God" (John 1:12, 13). A divine declaration constitutes us into God's children, bringing to an end our participation in the Adamic condition of death and sin.

Scripture describes our transfer from a fallen humanity to a reconciled one as a new birth. Believers are those who were "born of God" (1 John 3:9; 4:7). Jesus spoke about the experience of the new birth as "being born again," not through the weakness of the flesh, the natural birth, but through the power of the Spirit working in the life of the person (John 3:3, 5, 6). In fact, Paul adds that the old person, the one born in the Adamic fallen condition, has died, and that a new person has come into existence, an experience ritually enacted through the baptismal rite, by which believers are united to Christ (Rom. 6:4-6). When they were baptized the "old self was crucified" with Christ (verse 6) and they were resurrected to a new life in union with Christ. The new creation announced by the prophets has been inaugurated through the death and resurrection of Christ, and those who are in Him are part of that new creation (2 Cor. 5:17). They have put on the "new self, created to be like God in true righteousness and holiness" (Eph. 4:24). Christians are called to become what God has declared them to be. Consequently, Paul exhorts them, "Do not lie to each other, since you have taken off your old self with its practices and have put on the new self, which is being renewed in knowledge in the image of its Creator" (Col. 3:9, 10). Through the power of the Spirit the members of the new humanity no longer allow sin to reign over them (verses 4, 12).

Christ in us. To be "in Christ" is basically the equivalent of "Christ in us" (cf. Rom. 8:12; Col. 1:27; Gal. 4:19; Eph. 3:17). There is a kind of reciprocity between the two phrases that makes it impossible to acknowledge one without affirming the other. John uses the metaphor of a vine to express the two ideas in the context of the fruitfulness of the Christian life: "Remain in me, and I will remain in you. No branch can bear fruit by itself; it must remain in the vine. Neither can you bear fruit unless you remain in me" (John 15:4). In Galatians 2:20 Paul proclaims that he was crucified with Christ and that consequently he is no longer alive, "but Christ lives in me." The fact that Christ is in the believer demonstrates the presence of justification and points to the lordship of Christ in his or her life.

The indwelling of Christ occurs through the Spirit. We read: "The Spirit of God lives in you" (Rom. 8:9), He "is living in you" (verse 11), and God gives us life through the Spirit, "who lives in you" (verse 11). Christ empowers us through the Spirit to live a true life of service as new creatures. We can conclude that "life 'in the Spirit' is life 'in Christ' because the spirit is the presence of the resurrected, spiritual Christ. This is the basis for the vital union which exists between the believer and Christ."[8]

Conclusion

All the benefits of the atonement are available to us through the Son of God. We appropriate them in union with Him. That union takes place through the divine call to faith and salvation and our election in Christ, and expresses itself in the baptismal rite. The phrase "in Christ" places the emphasis on an intimate fellowship with Christ based on the recognition that He is Savior and Lord. Those who are in Christ belong to the new humanity inaugurated through Christ's redemptive work. They were born from above, through the Spirit, and are new creatures in Christ. For them the reign of death and sin—the natural condition of those who are in Adam— has come to an end. All of them have found in Christ the center of their lives.

---

[1] "To say that election took place before creation indicates that God's choice was due to his own free decision and love, which were not dependent on temporal circumstances or human merit. The reasons for his election were rooted in the depths of his gracious, sovereign nature" (Peter T. O'Brien, *The Letter to the Ephesians* [Grand Rapids: Eerdmans, 1999], p. 100).

[2] *Ibid.* One could say that God determined the existence of the church before the creation of the world (Ernst Best, *A Critical and Exegetical Commentary on Ephesians,* International Critical Commentary [Edinburgh: T. & T. Clark, 1998], p. 624).

[3] George W. Knight III, *Pastoral Epistles: A Commentary on the Greek Text* (Grand Rapids: Eerdmans, 1992), p. 375.

[4] Ellen G. White, "The Elect of God," *The Messenger,* Apr. 12, 1893.

[5] For a fuller treatment of the subject see, Ivan T. Blazen, *In Christ: Union With Him as Savior and Lord in Paul,* Biblical Research Institute Releases—2 (Silver Spring, Md.: Biblical Research Institute, 2005).

[6] M. A. Seifrid, "In Christ," in *Dictionary of Paul and His Letters,* p. 436.

[7] W. Elliger, "*En,* In, On, At," in *Exegetical Dictionary of the New Testament,* vol. 1, p. 448.

[8] Blazen, p. 10.

13

ATONEMENT AND
Cosmic Cleansing

The atoning power of the death of Jesus will reach cosmic dimensions as the conflict between God and Satan comes to its end. The Bible describes the final removal of sin and of the powers of evil from God's creation as a cleansing. In that sense it is the consummation of the work of atonement of Christ as sacrificial victim and high priest. As we have indicated, the Israelite ritual of the Day of Atonement typologically pointed to that important aspect of the work of Christ. We will briefly discuss the Day of Atonement in Daniel, the contribution of Hebrews, and the specific eschatological events that will result in a new heaven and a new earth free from the deadly miasma of sin.

Visions of Cosmic Cleansing

In the Old Testament the book of Daniel develops in a particular way the topic of the cosmic conflict and its resolution. It describes the rise and fall of kingdoms, their opposition to God and to His people, and their ultimate defeat. We are interested in the way the spiritual battle concludes. In describing the resolution of the sin problem Daniel takes the reader to the heavenly court of law (Dan. 7:9, 10, 26, 27) and to the Day of Atonement in the celestial temple (Dan. 8:13, 14). The two are closely related in that the Temple was also a place of judgment. The reference to the court of law indicates that the resolution of the cosmic conflict will take place in a heavenly legal and public forum and that the decisions made will be legally defensible and not arbitrary. Justice will prevail. The setting of the heavenly temple places the emphasis on the ultimate goal of the legal process, namely the removal of the unclean from God's creation and the restoration of harmony in the cosmos. The two are inseparable because the last could not be achieved without the first. In fact, as we already indicated, the Day of Atonement in the Israelite sanctuary services was a time of judgment.

In Daniel 7 the scene of judgment comes toward the close of the supernatural conflict and corresponds to the sanctuary scene in chapter 8, which also occurs toward the end of the cosmic struggle. Both scenes lead to the eschatological resolution of the cosmic battle. The judgment vindicates God's people, condemns their enemies, and fully clarifies to the universe God's involvement with the sin problem. It is to that cluster of ideas that the eschatological Day of Atonement speaks.

Daniel provides more information by placing the judgment/cleansing of the heavenly temple within the flow of history at a particular moment. The reference to the 2300 days in Daniel 8:14 points to the moment that the work of cleansing/judgment was to begin announcing that the cosmic conflict would soon come to an end. Contextual analysis allows the interpreter of the prophecy to determine the 2300-day period as beginning in 457 B.C. and ending in A.D. 1844. Many Christians consider that aspect of the apocalyptic vision offensive. Such an attitude is understandable although not acceptable. It is understandable in that those who have grown under the influence of the rationalism of modernism are unwilling to accept that a human being could be able to make predictions that received their fulfillment 2,300 years later.

But that attitude is not acceptable, because Scripture should determine the assumptions and presuppositions of the reader and not the other way around. The interpretation of that prophecy is not arbitrary. It has been reaffirmed on exegetical and theological grounds.[1] God placed those prophetic time periods in Scripture to help us understand where we are within His eschatological scheme of salvation and to motivate us to acknowledge the importance and the urgency of the times in which we live. The cosmic conflict is drawing to a close. The consummation of the work of salvation of Christ has begun in the initiation of His high-priestly work of judgment in the heavenly temple. In it He is fulfilling the antitypical service of the Day of Atonement.

Eschatological Day of Atonement in Hebrews

The eschatological interpretation of the Day of Atonement also appears in the New Testament. Cleansing as an image of atonement presupposes that we understand sin as a contaminating agent that needs to be removed in order to restore things to their pristine original state. This is particularly the case in the book of Hebrews, in which the image of cleansing reaches an important level of significance within salvation history. The idea that Christ has made purification for sins is central in the Epistle to the Hebrews.

Cleansing and the Day of Atonement in Hebrews. The book of Hebrews quickly introduces the idea of cleansing. The apostle writes: "After he had provided purification for sins, he sat down at the right hand of the Majesty in heaven" (Heb. 1:3). The passage describes two important events in the work of Christ for us. First, there is cleansing, and then the enthronement, or sitting down at the right hand of

God. The passage clearly suggests finality, the finishing of a particular task (cleansing) and the exaltation of the Son (the sitting down). But it does not elucidate how Christ effected purification. Concerning the second element, when we read it in the light of the rest of the book the sitting down should not be interpreted as resting from all work, but as the beginning of a work that is closely related to and that reveals the nature and meaning of the activity of cleansing.

Hebrews uses several expressions to explain the cleansing work of Christ in conjunction with His sitting down or enthronement: "But when this priest had offered for all time one sacrifice for sins, he sat down at the right hand of God" (Heb. 10:12). "[Christ] endured the cross, scorning its shame, and sat down at the right hand of the throne of God" (Heb. 12:2). We find in both passages the combination of the same two events found in Hebrews 1:3, one related to the sacrificial work of Christ and the other to His enthronement. In the first passage (Heb. 10:12), instead of using the word "cleansing," the apostle refers to the "one sacrifice for sins" offered by Christ. The second passage speaks of the sacrifice that Christ offered on the cross, indicating that the biblical author is interpreting His death in sacrificial terms. This suggests that His death is the instrument of cleansing. We could say that the sacrifice of Christ makes possible the cleansing and the forgiveness of sins (see Rom. 3:24-26). The cleansing/atoning sacrifice was offered once and for all and consequently Christ does not need to leave the presence of God to present an additional sacrifice. He can sit down as king. But then follows His ministry in the heavenly sanctuary (Heb. 8:2), directly connected to His work of mediation and cleansing.

Hebrews indicates that Christ's sacrifice has cleansing effectiveness in three related ways.

Cleansing of Sins Committed Under the First Covenant: "Now . . . he [Christ] has died as a ransom to set them free from the sins committed under the first covenant" (Heb. 9:15). The sacrifice of Christ legitimizes the cleansing performed in type in the tabernacle and the Jerusalem Temple. Thus His sacrifice on the cross forgives the sins of repentant sinners. It is a cleansing of past sins, committed under the old covenant as transgressions of the covenant law. This retrospective effect of the cleansing power of the sacrifice of Christ is not unique to Hebrews, but it is implied in other places in the New Testament (cf. Rom. 3:25; Acts 17:30).

Cleansing of Sin Today: The sacrifice of Christ continues to be effective for repentant sinners. As we have already demonstrated, Christ applies the cleansing power of the cross to those who find in Him their heavenly high priest: "The blood of Christ . . . [will] cleanse our consciences from acts that lead to death, so that we may serve the living God" (Heb. 9:14). The dead works from which we are cleansed "are the same dead works from which Christians are called to repent (6:1), and they contrast with the 'good works' that Christians are called to perform in love

(10:24). They are not works of the Law, but sins that defile the conscience."[2] This present cleansing is an intrinsic part of the intercessory work of Christ at the right hand of God (Heb. 7:25), and addresses not only our past sins but also the nondeliberate sins committed during our Christian pilgrimage (Heb. 10:26). In that journey we must "throw off everything that hinders and the sin that so easily entangles" (Heb. 12:1). It is through the power of the sacrifice of Christ on the cross, where He bore the sins of many (Heb. 9:28), that God forgives our sins. The Israelite system illustrated this through the daily services. The sacrifice of Christ fulfills the typological significance of the cleansing effected through the daily services.

Cleansing and the Antitypical Day of Atonement: The cleansing power of the sacrifice of Christ has also a future expression, represented by the cleansing ritual during the Day of Atonement, a typology present in Hebrews: "It was necessary, then, for the copies of the heavenly things to be purified with these sacrifices, but the heavenly things themselves with better sacrifices than these" (verse 23). It is true that the book does not *fully* develop the significance of that statement, but its mention indicates that the apostle had in mind an eschatological day of atonement. It shows continuity with the Old Testament, in which, as we have already argued, the ritual of the Day of Atonement pointed to a future eschatological day of atonement.

Sacrifice of Christ and the Day of Atonement. The immediate context of Hebrews 9:23 discusses the question of the sacrifice to be used in the antitypical day of atonement. In verses 25, 26 the thought briefly shifts from the sanctuary to that sacrifice, in order to explain why Christ's sacrifice is superior to those employed in the cleansing of the earthly sanctuary. The sacrifice is better because it is unique, which the author demonstrates by contrasting the sacrifice of Christ with those offered by the ancient high priest. The Aaronic high priest offered every year the blood of different sacrificial victims, but Christ did not appear before God to offer Himself again and again. That would be absurd, because it would have required Christ sacrificially to suffer many times since the foundation of the world. Thus the author established that the sacrifice of Christ is efficacious to deal with all the sins committed since the beginning of the world.

The conclusion is that Christ "appeared once for all at the end of the ages to do away with sin by the sacrifice of himself" (verse 26). He did not enter the heavenly sanctuary to offer Himself again and again, but to represent us before the Father. Christ offered Himself for us on the cross to remove the barrier that separated us from God—the cleansing mentioned in Hebrews 1:3—and from access to the heavenly sanctuary. It happened when He took our sin on Himself and died for us (Heb. 9:28). It is important to observe that verse 26 does not describe the sacrifice of Jesus in terms of the ritual of the Day of Atonement, but rather as a public manifestation, the purpose of which was to remove or "do away with sin."[3] The contrast is not between the entrance of Christ into the heavenly sanctuary to initiate the ritual of the antitypical day of atonement and the entrance of the high priest into the Most Holy Place of the earthly sanctuary during the Day of Atonement. Rather it is between the nonrepetitive sacrifice of Christ *on the cross* as a public display and the multiplicity of sacrifices offered by the high priest year after year during the Day of Atonement. The apostle discusses those sacrifices in order to illustrate the fact that the sacrifice of Christ is superior to the ones offered on those occasions because it nullifies sin once and for all, making it unnecessary to present another sacrifice for sin. The implication is that since the sacrifice of Christ is unique and final, there is no need to offer another sacrifice to cleanse the heavenly sanctuary. His sacrifice is better and more efficacious than those brought by the Aaronic priests. That single sacrifice is effective in the final resolution of the problem of sin.

Goal of the Day of Atonement in Hebrews 9:27, 28. Verses 27, 28 address the ultimate goal of the cleansing of the heavenly sanctuary. The author uses an illustration to emphasize the finality of the work of Christ as sacrificial victim, and in so doing introduces an idea central to the ritual of the Day of Atonement. "Just as man is destined to die once, and after that to face judgment, so was Christ sacrificed once to take away the sins of many people." The sacrifice of Jesus is as final as the death of a human being. He died once bearing the sins of many (see Isa. 53). The biblical author implicitly relates this to the cleansing of the heavenly sanctuary when he tells us that the Son of God took our sin on Himself, that is to say, He assumed responsibility for it.

The final judgment follows the death of a person, and in a similar fashion the sacrificial death of Jesus will be followed by something that is also unavoidable—the Second Coming. The reference to judgment may seem to be casual, but it is not. Judgment is closely related to the theological meaning of the cleansing of the sanctuary, as Daniel indicated, and the Second Coming. According to Hebrews the final judgment is a future event. Hebrews clearly states that "the Lord will judge his people" (Heb. 10:30). It is precisely at the Second Coming that God will reveal to all the decisions reached during the heavenly judgment (cf. Rom. 2:5). The judgment of God's people will result in their salvation or vindication,[4] as we find unequivocally stated in Hebrews 9:28: "Christ was sacrificed once to take away the sins of many people; and he will appear a second time, not to bear sin, but to bring salvation to those who are waiting for him."

That passage moves from the event of the cross (Christ bearing our sins) to the eschaton (the Second Coming). Christ fills that temporal gap with His high-priestly ministry "for us" in the heavenly sanctuary. Hebrews expresses the consummation of His work of salvation through two important ideas. First, at the moment of His return in glory His connection with sin will come to an end—He will appear "without sin." He dealt with the sin problem on the cross, as our sacrifice, and has been dealing with it in the heavenly sanctuary as our mediator, but that will conclude after He finishes His role of mediation before the Father. Second, He comes "to bring salvation to those who are waiting for him." This is the moment that the salvation of God's people will be consummated. At the Second Coming His people will be waiting for their High Priest to emerge from the heavenly sanctuary with eternal salvation for them. In the light of the rest of the epistle, this cleansing also looks forward to the establishment of the kingdom of God (Heb. 12:28; cf. Dan. 7), and to the moment that all the enemies of Christ, who have already been defeated (Heb. 2:14), will "be made his footstool" (Heb. 10:13). The last phrase points to "the final vindication of Christ wherein his enemies are fully and finally subjected to him."[5] This cleansing will result in an executive judgment "that will consume the enemies of God" (verse 27). That will be the final cleansing of the universe from the presence of sin and evil powers.

In Hebrews the cleansing of the heavenly sanctuary refers to the realities of the final judgment, the consummation of the salvation of God's people, and the ultimate defeat of evil powers. Thus the epistle unveils the typological significance of the Day of Atonement, enriching our understanding of the work of Christ for us.

Consummation of the Salvation of God's People

The resolution of the sin problem is complex and will be accomplished through specific, closely related eschatological events. It has an earthly dimension as well as a cosmic one. The earthly one deals with the people of God, while the problem of the wicked finds its resolution in conjunction with the fate of the cosmic evil forces. We will discuss both events.

Salvation of God's people. The return of Jesus in glory is for believers the most anticipated event in their Christian journey. It is their only hope in a world of omnipresent evil. They exist in constant expectation of the realization of that most wondrous hope. For them, to exist is to hope trusting in the reliability of the Word of He who told them, "I will come back" (John 14:3). For the children of God that moment is not a time of judgment in the sense of determining their final destiny, but one of vindication and of the revelation of salvation. Even before the appearing of the Son of God in the clouds of heaven they stand vindicated in the heavenly court. There their loving Savior will testify to their faith and deep commitment to Him in the midst of the most adverse and threatening circumstances. The heavenly tribunal calls their names in order to demonstrate that God, through Christ, was righteous and just and merciful in granting them forgiveness of sins and eternal life. The universe will recognize that their works of love were indeed the embodiment of a life of faith in Christ's atoning blood. The heavenly court will judge in favor of them, consummating their salvation in Christ (Dan. 7:22). The moment of the return of Christ is unquestionably one of salvation for them. The Lord comes, not to judge them, but to give them their reward of eternal life.

One can hardly anticipate the experience of the redeemed ones as they see their Savior approaching in heavenly splendor to take them home. That which for centuries God's people anticipated only through the eyes of faith will then be a reality to enjoy. They will be glorified through the power of the resurrected and glorified Lord. The lost glory of Adam and Eve will be finally restored to the human race in bodies free from the corrupting influence of sin and death. The resurrected dead members of the earthly family of God will join those still alive, and, shrouded in immortality, God will remove all from a world in which sin and evil reigned. The portals of eternity will open to them as the corrupting presence and influence of sin and death ceases forever. For them the cosmic conflict has personally come to an end. They are finally home.

The redeemed ones will participate in the resolution of the cosmic aspect of the sin problem. For 1,000 years they will judge the wicked and even the fallen angels (1 Cor. 6:3; Rev. 20:4). As they examine the heavenly records, they will witness the righteousness of God's legal verdict against the forces of evil. That cosmic judgment will vindicate the character of God in the eyes of those who remained faithful to Him throughout the history of sin and death in the universe. If there had ever been any doubts in their minds concerning God's love and justice, they will now be gone forever as they praise God for His righteous judgments against evil.

Resolution of the cosmic dimension of sin. God has still another dimension of the sin problem to resolve before there can be cosmic reconciliation. Satan, his fallen angels, and his earthly supporters need to join the heavenly family in recognizing the love and righteousness of God in dealing with the sin problem. While the wicked are dead as a result of the return of Christ (2 Thess. 2:8; Rev. 19:21), Satan and his angels have 1,000 years on our planet to reflect about their personal involvement in the crisis of sin (Rev. 20:2, 3). The millennium is an extremely important period of time in the divine plan for the restoration of the universe to peace. It is a period of transition from a world of death to one of life, from rebellion to ultimate harmony. As the powers of evil reflect over all that has happened, a process begins that will ultimately lead them to realize that they were mistaken and wrongly projected into God their own evil and absence of love. But at the end of the millennium, at the moment that God brings the wicked back to life (Rev. 20:5), they are not yet ready publicly to acknowledge it.

In a desperate attempt to regain control over the earth as their center of government, Satan and the wicked launch an attack against the City of God that has descended from heaven (Rev. 20:7-9; 21:2). As they rush it they find themselves confronting their own past. The heavenly books open before them, and they see their own lives and the role they played in the cosmic conflict (Rev. 20:11-13).

Unable to defend themselves against the charges and the evidence, they find that they can recognize only that they are guilty as charged. The cosmic warfare comes to an end—not just through persuasion but particularly through the surrender of the forces of evil to the Victorious King, Jesus the Lord. It is at that moment that their knees will bow down as they confess that Christ is unquestionably the Lord (Phil. 2:9-11). Now the cosmic controversy can come to closure. God's character stands vindicated even in the eyes of His enemies.

Satan, his angels, and their supporters can then be justly removed from the universe. Even though for a moment they resist surrendering their life, they finally do it, and God takes it from them. They will experience God's forsakenness and total abandonment as they succumb to the second death. The cosmic conflict is resolved in their own minds as they go into eternal death, fully persuaded that God was indeed love and that they were guilty as charged.

A cosmos at peace. The new creation that began with the incarnation of the Son of God and continued in the regeneration through the new birth of those who put their faith in Christ's atoning death now reaches its consummation in the re-creation of the earth. God permanently removes all traces of sin and death from it through the cleansing power of His purifying fire. John says, "I saw a new heaven and a new earth" (Rev. 21:1). The words of the prophet Isaiah are now fulfilled: "The wolf will live with the lamb, the leopard will lie down with the goat, the calf and the lion and the yearling together; and a little child will lead them" (Isa. 11:6). The universe now has perfect harmony—at its center the love of God displayed in the sacrificial life and atoning death of Christ.

It is indeed the cross of Christ that will make the universe secure for ever and ever and that will make impossible a resurgence of sin. The power of the atoning death of Jesus will not diminish through the passage of eternal ages, but will continue to increase, revealing new dimensions of meaning of the unfathomable depth of God's love toward His creatures. The redeemed ones will rejoice in the study of that topic and will continue to praise God and Jesus Christ for the magnificent gift of eternal life obtained for them at the cost of a divine *pathema*/suffering that they will never be able to understand fully.

Conclusion

The typological significance of the Day of Atonement symbolically pointed to the moment when Christ's work of redemption will result in the cleansing of the heavenly temple and of the universe. The purification of the sanctuary consummates the salvation of God's people, revealing that He had indeed been just and merciful in forgiving their sins and permanently deleting the record of them from the heavenly records. The work of atonement through Christ made it possible for them literally to join the heavenly family. The Lord returns in glory to take them home.

The cleansing of the universe from the mortal miasma of sin cannot take place until the forces of evil themselves acknowledge that they are guilty as charged and voluntarily bring their warfare to an end. The millennium prepares the way for the closure of the conflict and will lead to the recognition of the justice of God even on the part of the evil powers. At that moment sin and rebellion come to an end, overwhelmed by the unsearchable love of the Crucified One. The rest of the story is yet to be experienced in the context of eternity. We know at least one thing—that it will be an experience of eternal joy in the presence of loved ones and in the company of the One who loved us so much that He bore our guilt and death on the cross.

---

[1] The best source of information appears in the Daniel and Revelation Committee series, which includes such titles as Frank B. Holbrook, ed., *Symposium in Daniel* (Washington, D.C.: Biblical Research Institute, 1986); Frank B. Holbrook, ed., *70 Weeks, Leviticus, and the Nature of Prophecy* (Washington, D.C.: Biblical Research Institute, 1986); Frank B. Hol;brook, ed., *Issues in the Book of Hebrews* (Washington D.C.: Biblical Research Institute, 1989); Arnold V. Wallenkampf and Richard Lesher, eds., *The Sanctuary and the Atonement* (Silver Spring, Md.: Biblical Research Institute, 1989); and the articles "Divine Judgment" and "Sanctuary" in Raoul Dederen, ed., *Handbook of Seventh-day Adventist Theology* (Hagerstown, Md.: Review and Herald, 2000).

[2] Harold W. Attridge, *Hebrews* (Philadelphia: Fortress, 1989), p. 252.

[3] The Greek *eis athetēsis* (literally, "for the annulment/removal"), is a legal phrase meaning "declaration of annulment" (M. Limbeck, "*Atheteō,* Make Invalid, Declared Invalid," *Exegetical Dictionary of the New Testament*, vol. 1, p. 35). The preposition *eis* expresses goal or intended purpose. "The author recognizes that sin remains a force (12:1), but its binding condition has been abolished" (Craig R. Koester, *Hebrews* [New York: Doubleday, 2001], p. 422). There is an "already-not-yet" condition in the removal of sin. Although its removal is already a reality, its consummation is still in the future. We could suggest that the "removal of sin" is the equivalent to the redemption Christ obtained for us (Heb. 9:12) and His victory over evil powers (Heb. 2:14, 15).

[4] In Hebrews "God's people are not exempt from judgment (10:30), and in the New Jerusalem they will meet the God who is judge of all (12:23). Nevertheless, the author can urge listeners to remain faithful in confident hope that God's judgment will bring them salvation (4:9-10; 12:22-24) rather than condemnation" (Koester, p. 429).

[5] Donald A. Hagner, *Hebrews* (New York: Harper and Row, 1983), p. 141.

SUMMARY

In the Bible and in Adventist doctrine and theology the atonement is the final resolution to the cosmic conflict. The problem of evil and sin is not simply a human issue but one that has in some way touched the totality of God's creation. Its origin reaches back to a period of time before the creation of humanity. And yet its solution predates its origin. Long before there ever existed a creature, the Godhead planned the creation of intelligent beings and how to confront the possibility of evil. It was at that moment that God dealt with the problem of sin by formulating a plan that would unquestionably deal with it once and for all. The holy, just, merciful, and loving God, the Creator, was going to take the brunt of it personally, not because He felt responsible for it but because of His love for His creatures. The cost would be extremely high, namely, divine pathema.

For ages the divine plan remained hidden in the bosom of the Godhead. With the entrance of sin and death into the human family, the Eternal Three activated the plan formulated in eternity. In the Garden of Eden the full benefits of divine suffering were announced and made available to Adam and Eve and to all their future descendants. At the core of the plan was the decision to show grace, instead of divine rejection, to sinful humanity. God revealed elements of the plan in the experience of some of His servants (e.g., Abraham) and prefigured it in the sacrificial system. Even in Eden itself it became clear that God was going to provide a substitute, a Savior that would bear the penalty for sin in place of the sinner. The whole sacrificial system of the Old Testament was an anticipation and announcement of the coming Savior who would die for sinners. The priestly ministry illustrated how the Lord would deal with personal sin (daily services) and with the cosmic problem of evil (Day of Atonement). The different rituals pointed to atonement as a process by which the unclean and the holy came into contact, bringing as its result atonement and the forgiveness of sin.

The prophets proclaimed the coming of the Servant of the Lord (e.g., Isaiah), the Messiah who would arrive at a particular moment to atone for the sins of the people through His own sacrifice (e.g., Daniel). Isaiah announced in a magnificent way the experience and the work of the Savior. He described the rejection of the Servant by sinners and His substitutionary death as a sacrificial victim bearing the sins of all in order to grant them underserved righteousness. Those elements of the atonement, already revealed in the Old Testament, belong to the very nature of the atonement and must become a part of any discussion of the subject. What we should avoid is developing the topic of substitution in a way that undermines the unity of the Godhead and the love of God.

What the Old Testament announced and proclaimed became a reality in Christ. The costly sacrifice of God began at the moment of the incarnation of His Son. At the same time a new creation that was at peace with God irrupted into the old age of sin and death. In the permanent union of the human and the divine in the person of the Son of God, God was offering humanity a mediator through whom they could be also united to Him. Christ's whole ministry was a revelation of the grace and love of God calling humans to reconciliation with the Father and with each other. He was tearing down not only the barrier of sin that separated humans from the Father, but anything that could separate them from each other.

At the center of the divine plan for the salvation of the human race stood the cross of Christ. It was the means of redemption, reconciliation, forgiveness, expiation/propitiation, justification, etc. Scripture employs all those images in order to emphasize the richness of the sacrifice of Christ and how it solved the problem of sin in all of its manifestations and ramifications. On the cross God was actually taking upon Himself the penalty for the sin of the human race—that is to say, He was personally assuming responsibility for it. Since God was not in fact responsible for sin, the cross became a glorious revelation of His sacrificial love.

On the cross Christ experienced the penalty for our sin—namely, eternal separation from God. He became human to take our place and receive what was legally and justifiably ours in order for us to receive from Him what was legally and justifiably His. But it is at this point that the mystery of the atonement surfaces in all of its depth, setting limits to our understanding. We have suggested that because of the permanent union of the divine and the human in the Son of God, the separation of the human nature from the Father was at the same time the separation of the Son from the Father. It could not be any other way. The Son fully and uniquely experienced that abyss as it brought with it an indescribable sundering within the Godhead. God suffered as only God could suffer. He experienced the human penalty for sin in Himself. Consequently, the atonement is firmly grounded not in human suffering but in divine *pathema*.

Christ's resurrection, ascension, and enthronement in the heavenly sanctuary followed His death. As mediator before the Father, He is constantly applying the benefits of His atoning death to repentant sinners. However, human beings receive many benefits of His death independent of a faith relationship with Him. We have suggested that those gracious acts are the "common grace," used by the Spirit to summon humans to repentance. Those who accept the divine call are the chosen ones, and they receive through the mediation of Christ the fullness of the benefits of His atoning work. Through baptism they are incorporated into His saving event and are united to Him. Now "in Him," they belong to the new humanity instituted by Christ and not to the Adamic humanity of sin and death. They have been born again, and therefore they are a new creation.

The reconciling mediation of Christ in the heavenly sanctuary (the antitypical daily work of the priests) concludes with His work of judgment (the antitypical day of atonement). The resolution of the cosmic conflict will climax in a theodicy before the divine tribunal. It is through judgment that the forces of evil will be persuaded of the justice and mercy of God in the work of the atonement. The vindication of His people as well as the extinction of the wicked will provide the background for a cosmic proclamation of divine justice and love. Persuaded of the fact that they are guilty as charged, the forces of evil will surrender in the conflict in full recognition of the loving character of God. At that point the conflict will end and the cosmos will be cleansed of the destructive presence and influence of sin and evil. The originator of sin and all of those who chose to follow him will experience eternal death.

After that . . . eternity!

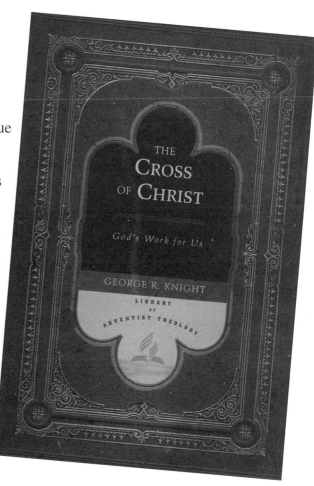

An Insider's Guide to the Book of Revelation

What exactly is the battle of Armageddon—and how will it affect us individually? Jon Paulien deciphers the clues found in the Bible to provide a clear understanding of this great battle and how the world will end.

978-0-8127-0477-8.

Paperback, 223 pages.

3 WAYS TO SHOP